Michael Kluckner and "Nº 8"

June, 1997

R. H. McMURRAY

The Pullet Surprise

[signature]
1998

The Pullet Surprise

A Year on an Urban Farm

TEXT AND WATERCOLOURS BY

Michael Kluckner

RAINCOAST BOOKS

Vancouver

FIRST PUBLISHED IN 1997 BY

Raincoast Books
8680 Cambie Street
Vancouver, B.C.
V6P 6M9
(604) 323-7100

1 3 5 7 9 10 8 6 4 2

CANADIAN CATALOGUING IN PUBLICATION DATA

Kluckner, Michael.
The pullet surprise

ISBN 1-55192-109-X

1. Kluckner, Michael, 1951- 2. Farmers — British Columbia — Langley — Biography. 3. Farm
life — British Columbia — Langley. 4. Farm life in art.
5. Langley (B.C.) — Biography. I. Title.

FC3845.L35K68 1997   971.13304'092   C97-910457-2
F1089.5.L35K68 1997

Design by Dean Allen
Project Editor: Michael Carroll
Copy Editor: Rachelle Kanefsky

Printed in Hong Kong

Raincoast Books gratefully acknowledges the support of the Canada Council,
the Department of Canadian Heritage, and the British
Columbia Arts Council.

Contents

⟨+ +⟩

Acknowledgements
<+ +>

Friends and neighbours appear as characters in a fictionalized form and in fictionalized episodes. Jan Tuytel and Ken Bose are real people, rather like the ones in the book. Christine Allen is my partner in agriculture, as in everything else.
My thanks to them all.

Introduction

⟨← ←⟩

*Diocletian's answer to Maximian is deservedly celebrated. He was
solicited by that restless old man to resume the reins of government,
and the Imperial purple. He rejected the temptation with a smile of
pity, calmly observing that, if he could show Maximian the cabbages which he had planted with his own hands at Salona, he
should no longer be urged to relinquish the enjoyment of happiness
for the pursuit of power.*

— Edward Gibbon, *The History of the
Decline and Fall of the Roman Empire*, 1783

"I CAN SEE WHY YOU MIGHT want to get out of the city, but I can't
understand why you'd want to tie yourself down with *animals*," a
friend had said to us. In fact, many friends said it. "Didn't your
daughter just move out?" they would ask. The friends were usually
employed in city jobs that offered a few weeks of freedom to travel
in return for 49 annual weeks of enslavement, but they had a point:
we *had* tied ourselves down with about a hundred new children,
although we were sure none of them would ever ask for the car keys.
We were from the city, yet we had gone farming.

Our exit from the city was a gradual one. Over the years we had
developed a pretty good idea of what country living might be about:
chopping wood, breathing fresh air, taking long walks on quiet
roads, perhaps grooming a recreational animal (a horse) — the
stuff of numerous "early retirement" ads, of articles in magazines

1

celebrating the get-away-from-it-all dream. In these modern times, we read, there was the option of being on-line with the stockbroker or of commuting by expressway to distant airports or skyscrapers for business. Implicit in this concept of living in the country was the fact that the money to sustain it would come from somewhere else.

We had also travelled, but had seen little in North America to nurture the dream. Commuting to a city job seemed environmentally suspect and stressful. Although city friends who had moved to the country had lots of peace and quiet — often too much of it — they didn't seem to do enough to connect with the land around them.

And what about farming? North American farms were huge, and they needed combines the size of condominiums and gangs of migrant labourers to make them work. However, in Europe, especially in the French countryside, we had seen the kind of place we were after: mixed farmyards of chickens and geese, some cows and sheep on pastures, modest lives lived in modest farmhouses, with the income from the *produits de la ferme* supplementing somebody's Foreign Legion pension. What they had was the family farm, of course, something that had existed in North America in my grandparents' time and still existed as a collective dream.

Farming like this promised to be somewhat different from the country living we had seen in the magazines and the ads. Yes, there would be wood chopping and we would probably have to buy a rider mower, but the fresh air would be mixed with the "dairy air" — the heady brew of aromatic agriculture. The long walks would not be on country lanes but along the fence lines to see where the coyote that ate the free-range chicken had gotten in.

In this anachronistic farming we proposed to undertake, everything would revolve around the changing seasons and the production of crops. We could cultivate a vegetable garden and put produce by for the long, cold winter. A crop might also be eggs, chickens, fleece, lambs, or the old-fashioned rosebushes Christine planned to raise. The options of telecommuting or being on-line with the proverbial stockbroker had to be there, for there was never really any question of making a complete living, whatever that meant, from the farm.

The place we found was in an "urban-shadow" area of dairying, horse breeding, poultry raising, and industrial-scale greenhousing and mushroom growing, and it cried out for new animals to fill its derelict barnyard. Among the remnants of what, a half-century earlier, had been a family-run dairy farm, were a fine old barn, a few abandoned outbuildings, and some mangers that looked like they were awaiting the second coming of Joseph and Mary and the three wise chaps. An almost-wild tabby cat, sleek from her diet of mouse and rat, slept on a dirty old sheepskin at the back of the barn. On the upper floor, where once loose hay had been stored for the winter, was a litter of dry, black pellets — the mixture of fur and bones and indigestible glop coughed up by barn owls. Along the roof's ridge, nearly 10 metres overhead, ran the track for the old hay hook; on the track, at the dark end of the barn, the owl sat silently.

Beyond the buildings, grassy meadows extended back to a neighbour's woodlot and the regular rows of grapevines of a small winery that occupied the hillside to the north. A double row of Lombardy poplars defined the driveway. Although the property was only four hectares, it seemed large to us and had around it properties of from two to 20 hectares, most of which, on the winter's day when we first saw them, harboured farm animals.

My 1913 copy of *Farm Management*, part of the rural textbook series once used in American schools, quoted Cato's 2,000-year-old advice to buy what others had built in order to "enjoy the fruits of another's folly." The place was perfect and, more to the point, it was affordable. We would not be throwing ourselves off the precipice into megadebt.

When the legendary family farm was at its zenith at the turn of the 20th century, the average one comprised about 30 hectares — the size a man with a couple of sons could successfully work. At that time, one farm family fed only three nonfarm families, which

3

was nevertheless a radical change from the situation a century before, when nine-tenths of the population were engaged directly or indirectly in farming activity. Even with the memory of hard manual labour fresh in the minds of most families, there was no shortage of books for dreaming urbanites. *Farm Management* noted the existence of titles such as *Three Acres and Liberty* and a popular poem called "A Little Farm Well-Tilled," but it also warned that "there may be less poetry, but there is a better living, in a large farm well managed."

That was then, when gasoline tractors had only just been invented, the plow horse was king, few farms had electricity, and even radio was still in the future. There was comparatively little to buy to fill up those farmhouse rooms, so "a living" meant little more than three square a day and a set of "Sunday go to meetin'" clothes for church and the funerals of fellow farmers who had been sucked into the steam-powered thresher. Life was simple. To round out his life, *Rennie's Agriculture in Canada*, published in 1916, advised the farmer to take a farm journal and a religious paper for Sundays, as well as a

daily newspaper, so he would not have "to go to the store or the tavern for the news of the day."

The 30-hectare family farm of the 1920s did not remain profitable for long; agribusiness, with its inorganic fertilizers and pesticides and herbicides, amalgamated huge acreages to raise monocultures of wheat or corn or animals. Windowless buildings housed vast flocks of chickens. It soon became rare to find an individual farm where the crops were grown to feed animals whose manure was then plowed back to fertilize the fields. The cycle of birth, death, and renewal — of sustainable agriculture — was becoming an anachronism. Farming was now truly an industry.

This industrial farming, and the supermarkets and long-distance trucking required to support it, have put the small family farm under siege. Unless they are breeding something exotic or growing organic food or herbs for a specialty city market that is willing to pay European-level prices, farmers on places the size of ours simply can't survive.

Moreover, there has always been city money and country money, as there are now the two solitudes of city people and country people. City money is tied to city expectations and city stress, and it is easy to make and even easier to spend. Country money comes slow and hard, but there is less opportunity to spend it, so it sticks around a little longer. An example: one of our lambs, born without any health problems, will grow to market size of about 40 kilograms in four months or so and can then be sold for about $100, three-quarters of which is "profit," meaning net income, as long as you don't factor in the cost of feeding the parents over the winter, the shed they live in, the fence that protects them, the investment in the land and the annual taxes, and the little bit of time every day required to care for them. Thus, you end up with $75 which, in the big city an hour away, will buy a reasonable dinner for two, two average tickets to an average game of the professional basketball or hockey team, or a couple of mediocre seats to see Rod Stewart the next time he's revived and put back on tour. A lamb equals two times two hours with Rod, and so on. Country money doesn't go very far when you take it to the city.

Before we moved to the farm, we considered buying weaned, castrated calves — steers, or beeves, as they're called — and pasturing them until they reached market weight, but their large size and bozo personalities put us off. We thought about milking goats and making chèvre, but quickly learned that a goat needs milking *every twelve hours* (like a cow, except they're even more fussy about the timing), and that in our part of the world you can't just make cheese and sell it at the farm gate — you need permits and inspections and a quota, unlike what we had experienced in the French countryside where a sign at the side of the road that read CHÈVRE would bring travellers to the door. One rumour said that piglets bought at the auction and fattened for market were the way to go, but after a neighbour described how one of her piglets killed and ate another, we rejected them, too. Sounds too much like Orwell, we thought. So we started with a few laying hens and progressed from there.

We had no illusions about what we were doing, and we knew that we fitted in somewhere between the family farms of the 1920s and the hippie back-to-the-landers of the 1960s. We proposed to farm with a small *f*, to provide ourselves with an educational experience, as it were, and to feed ourselves and the handful of people who bought our stuff. We knew it had as much to do with dreaming as it did with agriculture.

Roots

⟨+ +⟩

The farmer is the one vital factor in the world; even at this day we
would survive without iron and steel, gold, silver and copper, as did
our remote ancestors, but wheat, corn, oats, rye and barley from the
farm we must have that we may live.

— *The Dominion Educator,* 1923

ALTHOUGH THE CITY is the primary expression of sophisticated
humanity, it wouldn't have lasted a week without the bumptious
farmer. Until about the middle of the 19th century, almost everyone was concerned with agriculture, at least in part because most
people lived on farms or worked in related industries. Since then,
with mechanization and the vast increase in the productivity of the
individual farmer, most city people take their food supply for
granted and have turned their attention elsewhere. Today the happy
rustic of earlier times has to compete in a pluralistic world using the
language and skills of technology. Not just food is on the table —
prices, farmland preservation, production methods, animal rights,
and farm support and marketing boards are up for public scrutiny,
too. Following a bout of farmer bashing a few years ago, during
which government and media seemed united in the cause of removing farm subsidies and protective tariffs, a popular bumper sticker
in rural areas carried the admonition: "Don't criticize farmers with
your mouth full."

Only in recent years has the interrelationship of the city and its surrounding countryside been rendered optional by the ease of food storage and transportation. Whether in Europe, the Americas, or Asia, villages and, later, towns and cities arose concurrently with a primitive system of seminomadic agriculture that supplemented hunting and the gathering of wild foods. Domestication of animals, including dogs, cows, sheep, and pigs, and the crude cultivation of small plots of earth with hoes and digging sticks for the growing of grain allowed the prehistoric farmer to produce a small amount of food in excess of his family's needs — the essential element in creating a village, where there are people with occupations other than farming.

Cato, Pliny, Xenophon, and a score of lesser-known ancients wrote insightfully on agriculture, and the relevance of their advice today is illustrated by the quotations from their works scattered throughout this book. Later in the Western world, agriculture was still an acceptable interest for an educated man, encouraged by Renaissance writers like Thomas Tusser and Ulisse Aldrovandi, and extending into the 18th century with improvers like Jethro Tull, Thomas Jefferson, and Charles, Viscount Townshend. However, by Victorian times, when many of the problems of feeding the populace had been solved, a writer like the Reverend Edmund Saul Dixon felt obliged to include in his introduction to the *Treatise on the History and Management of Ornamental and Domestic Poultry* (1849) the caveat that "anyone claiming to be considered as an educated gentleman, may be thought to have done a bold thing in publishing a book on Poultry, and giving his real name on the title page." Agriculture was evidently no longer a subject for great minds.

Much of North American farming can trace its — uh — roots to northern Europe and the innovations of peoples such as the Belgae, a mixed Celtic-Germanic group who invaded Britain shortly before the Romans. Their development of a strong plow that was able to turn a rudimentary furrow established the long, narrow farm field familiar from images of medieval farming, such as the Limbourg brothers' *Les Très Riches Heures du Duc de Berry*, painted between 1413 and 1416. New words entered the language to describe the new techniques: a furlong, about 220 yards (200 metres), was a "furrow-long" — the distance a team of oxen could plow without a rest; an acre (two-fifths of a hectare) was a strip — a subdivision — of a field, about four poles or 22 yards (20 metres) wide by a furrow long, and was in theory the amount of land that could be plowed on a single day. The system worked out so that a 10-acre (four-hectare) farm was a furlong square — our little farm is square and just a fraction under a furlong on each side.

The farmstead that evolved during the Roman era continued into the Middle Ages, with variations from country to country depending on the power of the nobility and the oppression of the serfs. The example of England is not atypical: following the Norman conquest, the Saxon thanes were dispossessed of their land and most of the populace became little more than peasants, tied through the feudal system to the local lord of the manor, a baron, and thence to the king. The serf was up at dawn and worked until nightfall, year-round, with time off for the many religious holidays and feast days.

The village was often no more than a collection of 20 to 30 huts and cottages in which peasant families lived with their animals, a church, and the nearby manor house that stood with its barns and stables in the midst of a demesne or home farm. Cottages had their own garden plots, while the rest of the land was divided into crofts of a couple of hectares for individual tenants, and large fields for cultivation and grazing in common. There were usually three large fields farmed on a three-course crop rotation: one of wheat or rye to provide the community with bread, one of barley for ale (about four litres a day was the average consumption), and the third was fallow and grazed and manured by livestock. Sometimes vegetable crops were grown for winter fodder. Because there was little knowledge of plants and soil, this rotation was generally adhered to, even though it gradually depleted the land of its natural fertility.

9

Cattle were common, but because of the lack of fodder few could survive the winter, and most were slaughtered in the fall and salted down. Pigs, poultry, and sheep scrounged an existence around the village and in the nearby woods and usually met with the same fate as the cattle. The prize beast was the ox, which was harnessed into a team to pull the plow and gave milk and meat; it was cheaper to keep over the winter and had a quieter temperament than the horse. "Ther was no hors in the world so stronge That myght ffolowe hym a fur longe," wrote Sir Beues of Hamtown in the 14th century.

Because of wasteful seeding, losses to birds and field mice, and the lack of deep cultivation and proper drainage, crop yields were poor, about four to five times the amount seeded, which is about one-quarter the yield that farmers were able to expect in the 1940s and 1950s — the last decades when farming was still largely done on a traditional, sustainable pattern before modern seeds, fertilizers, and pesticides led to the Green Revolution. (Ken, the farmer I buy wheat and barley from, seeds about 45 kilograms per acre of wheat or barley and gets a yield of about 35 or 40 to one; on his organic fields, the yield is close to the same but his labour input is much higher, as it takes longer to spread manure than chemical fertilizer and to mechanically cultivate weeds than to spray them with herbicides. On the prairies, due mainly to lack of irrigation, grain yields are more likely to be in the order of 20 to one.)

The feudal system in England survived until the middle of the 14th century, although by that time the economy had evolved somewhat, with cash being required to pay rents and buy services. Following the plague year of 1348, labour was in very short supply and thus costly; the following year, in an effort to restore economic stability, Parliament passed a Statute of Labourers which, among other restrictions, froze wages. Other statutes followed, and in 1381 the peasants revolted; although the rebellion was put down, they eventually won most of their demands for the abolition of villeinage and manorial dues. The feudal lord, responding to these new rules and to economic changes occurring elsewhere in Europe, became a commercial landlord. The agent of this change was the sheep.

Between 1350 and 1550, vast tracts of former common land were enclosed by the English aristocracy for sheep grazing (Spain, with its merinos, was the only other country producing good wool). The poorest quality wool was used locally to produce coarse cloths such as kersey for the peasants' wardrobe, but the better quality went to Flanders and, later, to northern Italy where, today, fine architecture and a rich artistic legacy survive in cities like Brussels and Florence. Bruges, for example, had 40,000 looms in the 13th century; in 1421 the wool tax accounted for 74 percent of England's customs revenue. The process of enclosure of common land accelerated following Henry VIII's break with the Roman Catholic Church in 1534 and the seizure of the monasteries. During the Elizabethan era following Henry VIII's reign, many of the great country estates of England were built, and many English literary classics, by William Shakespeare and others, were written; the good times were due to the wool trade.

Throughout this period, peasants were driven from the land, then allowed to return to labour for wages. A yeomanry did evolve, however, and lived in slightly better circumstances than had the medieval serf. But there was little progress in agriculture – bad harvests brought actual starvation, while problems of storage and preservation reduced the amount of food available even in good years. The poor man often could not afford to eat his own poultry or eggs, as he had to sell them for cash while feeding his family on porridge with skimmed milk and maslin, a coarse bread made of barley and rye. Wheat flour was a luxury that was usually only found in the better houses, as was fresh meat. Poaching kept many alive through the winter.

During these years, three of today's common foods were introduced into Europe. The turkey was brought from New Spain to Old Spain in 1523 and was thought so odd that the English figured it had

come from Turkey, while the French thought it was from India —
d'Inde, ergo *le dindon.* The potato, a source of starch that had fed the
Inca civilization, was brought to Spain by a conquistador who had
harvested it in the Andes in about 1530. And corn, the maize of the
Americas, was grown by colonizers in New England and soon made
its way to Europe.

Real progress in agriculture began during the 17th century. A
royalist named Sir Richard Weston, who had taken refuge in Holland
during the English civil war, noted the practice there of growing
turnips for winter fodder and clover for hay. Both were sown late in
the year in fallow fields and served to enrich the soil while enabling
sheep and cattle to survive the following winter. Farmers began making silage — preserving root crops and grasses by packing them into
airtight mounds or silos, where natural fermentation preserved their
goodness (like sauerkraut). In 1701 a Berkshire farmer named Jethro
Tull invented the seed drill after having been frustrated by his
labourers' refusal to sow sainfoin (a haygrass like lucerne) in the
manner he wished. Following a visit to France, where he had
observed the local system of vineyard cultivation, he invented the
horse hoe. Using both of these implements, he was able to plant
grains and root crops at a controlled depth, using a quarter of the
previous amount of seed, and keep the land free of weeds afterward.

Another famous improver of the times was Viscount
Townshend, who resigned from Robert Walpole's cabinet in 1730
and devoted himself to agricultural experimentation at his estates in
Norfolk. He followed Weston's and Tull's suggestions and developed what came to be known as the Norfolk four-course rotation:
turnips, barley, clover and grass, and wheat. "Turnip" Townshend
promoted the Dutch practice of keeping animals alive through the
winter with turnips, and his crop-rotation scheme improved the
fertility of the soil so that crop yields increased. Diets generally
improved, even for the common people, with the result that the
population began to grow.

Concurrently English society was evolving so that the few landowners on great estates had many labourers working for a meagre amount of cash. In conquered Ireland in the 18th century, potatoes had become a staple crop: the cotters (tenant farmers) grew them for their own food while growing grain and raising cattle to pay the rent. The potato crop failed first in 1739; in search of higher yields, cotters selected only a few strains and inadvertently narrowed the genetic base to the point where there was little protection against blight. The crop failed again, to greater or lesser degrees, in 1816, 1821, 1822, 1831, 1835, and 1836; in spite of this record, as the years went by the Irish became increasingly dependent on potatoes, supplemented with milk and a few vegetables. In 1845 the potato crop failed all across Europe, and 2.5 million people died in the famine.

The enclosure of common lands continued in England into the 19th century. In tandem with the Industrial Revolution, enclosure forced small farmers off the land and into the cities or, as was the case especially with the Irish, onto ships bound for North America. Essayists, including Samuel Laing and William Cobbett, wrote despairingly of the effects of industrial development on the English working classes, the loss of their common land and their traditional skills, and their bitter poverty. The wars against France, from 1793 to 1815 during the Napoleonic era, had forced England to become self-sufficient in food, forcing out the old order of village farming that had been based more on hierarchy than efficiency. But for those who were able to hang on, new markets appeared, serviced by the railways that allowed farmers to ship their produce quickly into the cities. The English landscape of hedgerows, fields, and farms that is familiar today evolved as a direct consequence of the wool trade and the Napoleonic blockade.

In North America, with its abundance of land and absence of a landed gentry, the dream of a farming yeomanry took root. The contrast between the situation in the New World and that in the Old World was well described by Thomas Jefferson, who wrote in 1782 that agriculture was not what it might be because of "our having such quantities of land to waste as we please. In Europe the object is to make the most of their land, labour being abundant; here it is to make the most of our labour, land being abundant." In Jefferson's day, nine out of 10 Americans were engaged in farming and food production.

Settlers in the United States and Canada were pushing westward into new valleys and seeking to carve out their independence on the land. A flurry of inventions in the first half of the 19th century revolutionized farming and began the process of its mechanization. Among these were improvements to the plow, most notably a self-polishing steel model built by the blacksmith John Deere in 1837: its mouldboard was curved enough that it did not have to be pulled out of the furrow and cleaned with wooden paddles, and it was strong enough to break the sod of the midwestern prairie. A few years earlier, in 1831, Cyrus Hall McCormick had successfully demonstrated a horse-drawn reaper; three years later, he patented it. And in 1844, in Racine, Wisconsin, Jerome Increase Case began to manufacture a steam-powered threshing machine, replacing the age-old tradition of threshing grain with flails or the hooves of horses or oxen on the floor of the barn and winnowing it in the breeze. Forever after, much of the farmer's capital and income went to buy equipment rather than to pay wages. Thus, while the farmers' productivity and prosperity soared, the number of North Americans employed on farms slowly declined, from more than four-fifths in 1820 to less than one-half by 1855. McCormick, for one, profited greatly from the California gold rush, as many farmers were deserted by their workers and had to mechanize to harvest their crops. Steam-powered tractors were introduced in 1858, but they were used mainly for hauling threshing machines to the fields and powering them.

One of the world's largest farm-equipment companies began in Daniel Massey's blacksmith shop in Ontario in 1830. Massey had imported a clumsy mechanical thresher from the United States and, with his son Hart, modified it into a more usable machine. Over the next 30 years they improved on other firms' ideas, adapting them for the rougher terrain of Canada; with some firms, like the Harris Company of Brantford and the Toronto Reaper & Mower Company (which had designed but been unable to market a twine binder for grain), Massey bought them out or amalgamated with them. Massey-Harris machines became popular all over the world; in 1953 the firm merged with Irishman Harry Ferguson's company, which had developed a line of lightweight tractors and perfected the hydraulic control of implements.

For a relatively brief period – say, from 1870 to 1930 – all of the elements of cheap land, available labour, affordable implements, and readily accessible markets came together to create a heyday for the family farm (in England the period known as "high farming" started at about the time of the Crimean War, 1853, but continued only until the 1870s, after which the country resumed importing most of its food). Most were truly *family* farms: a 1912 study by Cornell University of 947 farms in New York found that only four percent of them were run by a single person, many of whom were widows or widowers with for-sale signs up. A 1930 study showed that one-quarter of Americans lived on or from the farm, and that only 40 percent of those were tenant farmers. This compared with a mere seven percent of the British work force who were employed in agriculture, and nine out of 10 of them were tenant farmers. In the Canadian West, farmers brought out to the newly opened prairies by the railways battled the climate and tough sod to carve out huge wheat and flax operations; although many of these were large, capital-intensive farms, an elaborate marketing system through the Canadian Wheat Board helped make them profitable.

Inevitably, though, crop production by family farms began to go the way of the traditional craftsman, and farming became industrialized. The crucible for much of the change was the American West, most notably California, where fruit for canning, lettuce, and cotton required a peasantry – a permanent underclass – bound to the large estates. Cotton had, of course, been the primary crop of the antebellum era in the southern United States, but the California experience was different in that the large estates that were run with a small permanent staff required a throng of migrant workers for the four stages of chopping, hoeing, irrigating, and picking. In the 1920s, a four-hectare hop ranch with 12 full-time employees required 500 workers at harvest time.

But of all the crops grown in California, lettuce was the most precarious, its cultivation described by historian Kevin Starr as "a high-wire act of time and money." Because lettuce had to be harvested, trimmed, and packed by hand at the precise time it ripened in order to arrive still fresh at the market (which might be almost two weeks away by refrigerated railway car in the eastern United States), the business became highly centralized and coordinated, and the farmworkers highly regimented yet mobile, unlike the medieval serfs who died within sight of the huts where they were born. A new type of peasant evolved: gangs of farmhands in Model Ts worked through the season from Texas to Canada, travelling from county to county and crop to crop. By the 1920s in California, a permanent population of Filipino and Mexican farmhands worked the Imperial Valley throughout its growing season from fruit to cotton to lettuce.

However, most other crops – wheat, for example – relied on mechanization for their harvest. As early as the 1880s, steam tractors and combines dominated the Sacramento Valley, and in 1901 it was estimated that a wheat combine in four minutes did the reaping, binding, and threshing that took nearly three hours of a man's time. The shortage of farm labour became a permanent problem. Following the social dislocation of the First World War, fewer people were willing to have their horizons prescribed by the conditions of their birth; as reflected in the soldiers' song, "How You Gonna

Keep 'Em Down on the Farm, After They've Seen Pareeeee?", people struck out for the cities and new opportunities. Some said that the Model T would liberate the farmer and end his isolation, but if anything people drove away from the farm and didn't go back. One of the last crops to be mechanized was the tomato; it awaited the development of the tough-skinned, mellifluously named VF145-B7879 at the University of California campus at Davis. Eventually tomatoes were picked green by machine, shipped, and then reddened (rather than ripened) by ethylene gas.

Increasingly the risk and investment in crops such as lettuce and cotton demanded consistent and efficient applications of fertilizers and sophisticated methods of weed and disease control. As described later, in the chapter entitled "The Pullet Surprise," poultry farmers at Petaluma had already blazed the trail by industrializing the laying hen. The first pesticides were introduced onto American fields in 1924, although DDT, invented by a German chemistry student in 1873, was not used in North America until 1943. Two years later, the American Chemical Paint Company patented 2,4-D — developed by E. I. du Pont as a war weapon — as a selective plant killer that destroyed many common weeds while leaving food crops such as corn and wheat alone. Chemical fertilizers were put into common use at the same time, and equipment manufacturers increasingly developed implements specifically for the new agricultural chemicals. With all this new investment, the farmer had no choice but to grow (bigger) and specialize. Traditional fertilizers, such as chicken manure, had no role to play on these modern farms, and instead of being a boon, they often became a nuisance and a pollution source.

Changes in urban society reinforced and supported the trend toward specialized agriculture and concentrated control. Processed convenience foods, such as Kraft's Velveeta, Miracle Whip, and Cheez Whiz, introduced respectively in 1928, 1933, and 1953, found ready markets with busy families. War work by women, and by former servants, reduced the time available for traditional home cooking. The early 1930s had seen the introduction of the self-service grocery store, and by the late 1930s the A & P, Humpty Dumpty, Safeway, and Loblaw's used shopping carts and mass advertising to capture a major share of the market. By 1940 15,000 American stores were equipped to sell frozen food, a 30-fold increase over the previous decade. Concurrently the way people shopped had changed: universal car ownership and major public expenditures on roads prompted the creation of supermarkets, and then supermarket chains, which bought products centrally and supported the new farming system. By 1952 the typical American grocery store carried about 4,000 different items, compared with fewer than 1,000 two decades before. The successful introduction of the TV dinner in 1953 reflected a wholesale change in the way families ate their meals.

To meet this domestic demand, and to grow food for the lucrative export market, farmers selected only the most productive types of grains and other crops like corn to grow commercially; in dairying, where nearly all the cows today are Holsteins, a similar genetic focusing has occurred. In 1970, in an event reminiscent of Ireland in the 1840s, much of the corn crop failed due to a fungus. Some of the very toxic early pesticides, including DDT and the chlorinated hydrocarbon insecticides like dieldrin, have been banned, but modern pesticides and herbicides are considered essential by most farmers for most crops; similarly some growth hormones and antibiotics have been banned, but newer, more refined ones are critical to maintaining levels of production. Into the mix has been added bovine somatotropin (BST), a synthetic hormone used to increase milk production in dairy cows, and mammal proteins in livestock feed, which led to the outbreak of mad-cow disease that all but destroyed the British beef industry in the mid-1990s. And in spite of the Green Revolution of high-yield crops, worldwide grain reserves are at historic low levels. It is all rather like a high-tech version of the Middle Ages, where agricultural science does a ritualized dance to keep ahead of restless, inventive Mother Nature.

If that is all a dark cloud, the silver lining is the new, niche market that has opened up for organic and natural food, grown on a small scale and sold at a premium price in city markets catering to the affluent and the particular. Throughout North America, family farmers are scratching out a living with rare breeds, heritage seeds, and sustainable farming techniques. One crop with a good premium market is the tomato, as the sophisticated urban palate searches for an alternative to the bland flavour of the commercial, artificially reddened product. Often small-scale farmers supplement their incomes by selling the farm experience – harvesting picnics, visits during lambing, and roadside vegetable and egg stalls – to urbanites out for the old-fashioned Sunday drive. Much of it seems like hobby stuff – lifestyle enhancement, perhaps – beside the big, sleek operations that provide raw materials to food processors and produce to supermarket chains, but many of the new, individual farmers are treading lighter on the land and keeping alive the broad genetic base of plants and animals. If history is anything to go by, that will be important in the future.

The city and the country are two solitudes; many city people take the stability of their food supply for granted and direct their concern toward the fate of the natural environment and wild animals rather than to the human-influenced agricultural environment and domestic animals (too many country people, perhaps, are indifferent to whether farming is done in an environmentally sustainable way). There is the additional question of whether the aesthetic quality of the countryside conforms to city people's ideals, and whether farmers lose political support for farm subsidies and farmland preservation because so much of modern agricultural production occurs in an aesthetic wasteland of chicken batteries and feed lots.

Even in areas of small holdings, such as the one where we live, the amount of specialization is astonishing. We live within sight of a large park that is laced with horse trails, and many of our neigh-bours keep horses and board them for city people. The road in front of our farm is a dead end, and so it is popular with riders who want to cool their horses down after a gallop in the park; generally these horse people have an aloof demeanour, especially when in the saddle, and walk or trot down the road past us without acknowledg-ing our presence. But horses have minds of their own, and if they see something they don't understand they will often stop dead in their tracks. The hapless rider, who generally would like to be in control, can often do little until the horse has satisfied itself that all is okay.

One day, when Christine was gardening near the front gate, she looked up to see a horse, with rider, standing stock still and looking up the driveway. "Can I help you?" she asked.

"Oh, it's all right, I think," the rider replied. "It's just that my horse has never seen a chicken before."

Mixed Messages

⟨← ↔⟩

One great advantage of farming as compared with city life is that the farm furnishes work for children. Under modern conditions there are thousands of children who are more in need of a chance to work than of laws to prevent child labor.

— G. F. Warren, *Farm Management,* 1913

MANY OF TODAY'S most committed urbanites have farms in their pasts. For some the memories of childhood on a farm – the smell of chicken manure on a hot day, an aggressive gander, poverty (perhaps) and isolation, the endless repetition of chores – are so unpleasant that paradise becomes, say, a sidewalk café, even if diesel taxis and buses are idling nearby. But for those of us who grew up in the city, there was just imagination, fuelled by cartoons, magazine articles, art, and literature, to help us form an impression of the countryside. The reality of agriculture was not something we had to bother with.

I was a city child, like the vast majority of North Americans on an urbanizing planet in the 1950s and 1960s. Vegetables were objects laid out in display cases in the supermarket, stripped of tattered leaves and washed clean of slugs and soil. Meat was a grey lump wrapped in brown butcher's paper, frozen like one of Sir John Franklin's sailors in the frosty arctic of the deep freeze, or a plastic-covered slab swimming in thin, bloody fluid on a Styrofoam tray. I'm not sure if I had ever seen a vegetable growing, except for corn and cabbages in distant fields as we streaked by in the car, and I had never seen anything dead, except for a robin killed by the neighbour's cat, which we buried in the backyard with full Anglican liturgy.

Like most urban children, I formed my impression of farms from storybooks. Old MacDonald had a farm (ee-eye-ee-eye-oh) where a great variety of animals lived and sang in chorus at feeding time; The Little Red Hen tried to talk the other farmyard animals into helping with the chores, but ended up having to do it all herself; Chicken Little was unable to convince the other animals that the sky was falling, although she may have been speaking metaphorically; Beatrix Potter's Jemima Puddle-Duck and Tom Kitten had their adventures with the other animals and coexisted, if a bit apprehensively, with the furry and feathered wild things that lived in burrows or hedgerows. On television Foghorn Leghorn dominated his barnyard and was certainly a match for the big "dawg" there, and although Walt Disney cartoons were usually pretty dumb, the farm animals always had *personalities*. They weren't ciphers, and so from a very early age I believed that farm animals were pretty much right up there on the intelligence scale with the clever, free, wild animals that inhabited the forests and fields of my imagination, and so deserved respect and a decent quality of life.

Along with this imagined image of animals came a mental map of the farm. Whether illustrated in a picture book or described in text, all these farms were comprised of a collection of barns, coops, and shacks where the different critters lived. On the cover of the *Saturday Evening Post,* Norman Rockwell's oil paintings depicted an idealized farm life: rosy-cheeked children waiting patiently at a laden Thanksgiving dinner table, spotty boys with red arms and necks but white bodies skinny-dipping in a pond, teenage girls flirting on party-line phones while the whole district listened in. The isolation hinted at from time to time in these pictures seemed only to heighten the experience of home and place, which even in the city of my childhood was becoming a little tenuous.

And then there was "serious" art and literature. Agricultural art was often romantic, like John Constable's English landscapes, or folksy, like Thomas Hart Benton's American farm paintings, and only occasionally grim, like the Frenchman Jean-François Millet's *The Gleaners*. Thomas Hardy's Tess Durbeyfield lived in a bucolic Wessex countryside where, indeed, people worked hard for little material reward, but where the aesthetic and moral quality of life was infinitely superior to that in the smoky factory towns not far away. D. H. Lawrence's Paul Morel in *Sons and Lovers* courted Miriam on a small family farm described in exquisite and loving detail: the wildflowers along the ditches, the low evening sunlight pulling long shadows from the oak woods while a colliery glowed on a distant hillside. But then there was John Steinbeck's *The Grapes of Wrath* and the members of the hapless Joad family, who were all but destroyed by an agricultural system that had turned them into migrant workers little better off than slaves.

As a child I spent summers at a cabin on a lake, and my mother, who had grown up on a stump farm during the Depression, negotiated for corn and peas, beans and berries with the local farmers. Toward the end of the summer, a travelling circus came to the nearby town, and on Saturday night a dance in the big hall on the fairgrounds emptied the surrounding countryside. In my memory, the farm boys looked awkward on the dance floor, uptight, dangerously on edge after the weeks of hard work in the boiling summer sun. Always there were fistfights and brief wrestling matches in the dust just out of reach of the yellow shaft of light that spilled out the door from the dance floor.

When I was 18, on a summer break between university terms, I got a job with the electrical utility in a farming valley a few hundred kilometres from my city home. I worked from an office on the dusty main street of a little market town in the midst of a sea of apple orchards and took lodgings in a run-down house nearby. After a week or so, when I had tired of Kraft Dinner on my hot plate and the greasy burgers dished up at the café, I heard that a widow named Jean Brown was willing to take a boarder for the summer. On the phone she said I could stay as long as I caused no trouble, so at lunchtime I walked the half mile along the main street and up a side road, past orchards and a few houses, to a driveway marked by a large pine tree. At the end of the driveway, behind a well-tended kitchen garden and a lilac hedge, stood a farmhouse that was probably 50 years old. This was Jean's place. A low, unpainted wooden building that seemed to grow out of the sandy hillside behind the house was her root cellar. I could see a footpath winding its way up the hillside through the scattered pine trees and disappearing over the top. I soon discovered that it led to the home of Edwina Schneider, a farm wife of fundamentalist beliefs who remained Jean's friend as long as she didn't talk religion.

One Saturday morning, as I was slumbering while the smell from the nearby chicken plant wafted through the open window, I awoke to hear conversation downstairs. Remembering that Jean disapproved of late sleepers, I dressed hurriedly and, blinking and scratching in the bright morning light, descended the steep, narrow staircase to the kitchen. At the table was Edwina, holding forth.

"Oh, good," she shrilled before I had a chance to mumble a good morning. "A *man*! I've got some kittens that need to be drowned."

"*Need* to be drowned...?" I repeated. "Sorry ... not me...."

"Oh," she said, with her chicken eye fixing a sharp stare on me, as if I could use a good peck. "City boy." Dismissing me with a wave of a hand, she said: "Never mind, I'll get somebody else," and went back to regaling Jean with the latest gossip from the surrounding farms.

They were *country* people, as in the old saying, "you can take the boy out of the country, but you can't take the country out of the boy." Country meant unsentimental and practical, two of the characteristics that the soft urban life had bred out of humans like me.

Some years later I found a better balance between soft and hard on a small farm in Australia, in a town called Quirindi, half way between the tropical coast and the baked outback. The owner was Christine's cousin, Doug, a former stockman and rodeo rider who, as his family grew, gave up the weeks in the saddle for the less-punishing farm-insurance business. But they had maintained a small farm on about 10 hectares along a creek that was all but dry in the summer drought. Their household drinking water came from a galvanized metal tank attached to the side of the house, which collected water from the spreading tin roof during semiannual downpours. In the farmyard and out on the fields were about a dozen sheep, a cow, several horses, some turkeys and chickens, and a pair of beautifully trained Border collies that rounded up whoever needed rounding up. According to the family rule, any animal could be named that wasn't going to be eaten. The working dogs were only fed by Doug and could not be petted or played with — their role was to work. All the other animals had roles, too, and were in a sense treated equally, except that some lived longer than others.

We slept in a tent a little ways from the house, near the gum trees that lined the dry creek. Every morning, as the sky brightened into a pastel turquoise in anticipation of the sunrise, a dawn chorus in glorious surround-sound serenaded us. A rooster crowing a ways to the east was echoed by another far off to the north. Sheep baaed. A cow in the distance began the grunting moo that is a hilarious imitation of a certain sexual experience. Far away a dog shouted. And in the trees above us the birds twittered and cawed, billed and cooed. It was magical! We *had* to have a farm some day, we agreed.

The years inched by. Finally we were able to get our piece of green heaven, and we closed the deal at the beginning of winter. It was to be ours in March. We knew it meant a certain level of captivity — we wouldn't be able to do any significant travelling, at least until we managed to get everything running smoothly. With that in mind, we put everything into storage and, with a suitcase each, got on a plane to Paris, picked up the train to Marseilles, bought a car, and spent a few months meandering around the countryside of France and Italy. There were young goats in fields and old goats in the bars, *polli ruspanti* (free-ranging chickens) scratching around Tuscan farm-yards, and shepherds grazing their flocks in the olive groves and moving them to fresh pastures along the narrow country roads.

As February drew to a close, we returned with our wanderlust sated and prepared to become stay-at-home country folk.

Serf and Turf

⟨+ +⟩

Even though the earth lie waste and barren, it may still declare its nature; since a soil productive of beautiful wild fruits can by careful tending be made to yield fruits of the cultivated kind as beautiful.
— Xenophon, *Oeconomicus,* c. 375 B.C.

It was a rainy day in March when we moved to the country. The snow that had hung around for much of February, while we were still dawdling our way northward through Italy, had gone, leaving the previous autumn's long grass matted and grey on the back pasture. Our worldly chattels, in storage in a container for three months, arrived on a trailer too long to make the turn into the driveway so that everything had to be lugged the hundred metres from the gate to the house. Then a storm blew in, taking down a tree somewhere and knocking out the electricity and telephone for 24 hours — an inauspicious beginning to a new life if ever there was one. However, over the next several days, the world ever so slowly began to turn green, as needle-thin shafts of fresh grass pushed their way through the soggy thatch. Winter was over and spring was a-comin' in.

Dotted about the pasture were clumps of a sedge, or was it a reed — tufts of tough green spikes as much as a metre tall — that looked like they belonged in a swamp. And they did! A tour of inspection confirmed that the pasture was indeed a swamp, the soil sour from being constantly soaked, a perfect habitat for swamp grasses and mosquitoes. In a low spot in the middle of the field, the water was standing even taller than the tops of my duckies (the low-rise, slip-on rubber boots beloved of farmers, although designed for the sole purpose of sandpapering the ankle bone – the podiatric equivalent of a hair shirt). As I slopped along, feet cold and socks now wet, I disturbed frogs among the reeds, and a pair of mallards burst into flight from behind a tussock several steps away.

Returning to the house, I fished out the legal documents that had been part of the purchase of the farm. Included with the survey was a reproduced piece of an old map from the 1920s, which showed a dotted, curved web of lines across the back pasture that seemed to indicate a watercourse. The winery and the fields to the north were high and dry, and below us to the south across the road, on the far side of our neighbour's cattle-dotted field, was a real stream, probably once fed by our little watercourse. It appeared that our rill had silted up or maybe been filled, but it had never been properly drained into a ditch. No wonder the cattle we could see in the distance looked as if they ought to be wearing galoshes.

"Proper drainage of the land forms the very basis of successful agriculture," wrote William Rennie in 1916. "The soil may be ever so rich, but without sufficient drainage, either natural or artificial, its production can never reach the limit of what is possible." With the removal of the surplus water of early spring, Rennie explained, the ground became more porous and better able to hold water in the dry summer; drier soil was warmer soil, encouraging bacteria to break down organic matter. Money spent on drainage was the best spent money on a farm.

The physical condition of our new farm slowly began to make sense. The original farmer had had enough money to build a fine barn and the outbuildings necessary for his small dairy operation and, owning a more extensive property than the four hectares we had bought, he had hayed his highest, driest fields for winter feed. But, over the years, the place had been subdivided and changed hands, the most recent owner having modified the barnyard into a feedlot for Charolais cattle. In this new setup, the one we had inherited, a post-and-beam shed of about 10 metres by 20 metres had been built onto the side of the barn to provide winter shelter, and the ground under the shed and around the barn had been covered with a thick layer of grooved concrete. Under the shed roof, layers of sawdust and bedding straw, mixed with manure, had been pounded by the cattle's hoofs into a material with the consistency of plywood. This was known as daub, the manure-and-straw mixture of medieval wattle-and-daub houses that in Europe have demonstrated their ability to survive for centuries.

Evidently the state of the fields hadn't bothered our predecessor, as he had brought in grain by truck and fattened and "finished" his cattle on the concrete feedlot. Low, wet spots in the fields had no doubt become disposal sites for the manure he had no use for, as he was not growing any crops or doing any serious pasturing of his animals. A pile of ancient steer manure, about enough to fill a large house's living room from floor to ceiling, occupied one corner of the feedlot and provided nourishment for a thicket of stinging nettle and thistles. A cattle chute — two lines of rail fence a cow's width apart — stood beside the barn, scarcely visible amidst some overgrown elderberry bushes. Only a stud service in Alberta remembered our predecessor's farm and continued to mail a glossy publication containing colour pictures of prize bulls of a number of different breeds (Charolais, Blonde d'Aquitaine, Aberdeen Angus, Hereford, and so on), giving their ancestry and vital statistics, most notably their scrotal circumference, and offering to send semen by post.

To us the state of the pasture was a problem. There was no visible beginning or end to the old stream course, but the topography was putting a lot of water onto our place. Then, suddenly, the proverbial light bulb went on — we could dig a pond in the back pasture and drain the excess water off the field into it! How simple! Wildlife habitat! Or irrigation! Perhaps a swimmin' hole, à la Norman Rockwell! Maybe winter skating parties, too!

29

Looking for advice on what to do and what to plant around it to attract wildlife, Christine phoned the government agency that we figured would be responsible for ponds. The grave voice on the other end cautioned her that permanent bodies of water larger than a bathtub had to go through an approval process, that neighbours and environmental officials would have to be notified and a hearing held. At her expressions of dismay, his voice took on a sympathetic tinge. "You never heard this from me," he said, "but in my experience, it's easier to beg forgiveness than to ask permission." And he hung up. So it was decided — we would do whatever it was we were going to do, employ Midnight Pond Supply or whoever, but our project had nothing to do with pond making. We were swamp deepening.

The classified ads at the back of the local newspaper contained a section of "Farm Services" and notices by a few people who dug trenches, tilled fields, spread manure, and performed the other services we would no doubt require at some point. However, phone calls to them drew little response, other than vague promises to drop by and look at the problem at some indeterminate time in the future when they had cleared away the backlog of work created by all the rain. Like Fred Astaire and Ginger Rogers during the Great Depression, these people were making money when times were bad.

A little discouraged, we stood at the back window of the house and gazed to the north across our soggy meadow toward the higher ground. On our neighbour's big field, the one separating our place from the winery, a flock of sheep moved slowly about, nibbling at the new grass shoots. There were newborn lambs: twins sleeping in a little woolly bundle on the dry grass at one spot, a black one sticking close to its mother at another. In the distance, past the winery about a kilometre away, a big machine was working — a digger on Caterpillar tracks with a shovel bucket on the end of a long boom, the sort of thing used in cities to tear down heritage buildings and affordable housing. Perhaps this was what we needed to dig the pond.

I walked up late in the afternoon and introduced myself to the operator, name of Ed, who it turned out was redoing the septic field on his own place. Usually, he explained, he contracted out to municipalities laying gas or water pipes, but with a large job just finished he was taking the opportunity to catch up on work at home. We talked for a while about the weather, politics, and our individual lives and families, while I fidgeted a bit — my attitude was still a city one, where you get down to business right away, while Ed lived on country time, which meant that he took the opportunity to chat when a human came by.

Ed was about 55, or maybe 45, middle height, solid build, jeans and jean jacket and ball cap. He had grown up in the area and told me with some pride that he had been a bad boy in the local school, excelling only at boxing. One day in grade 11, pushed past the limit of his temper by a teacher, he had taken a swing at him — Ed wasn't specific about any damage he did. Without waiting to be expelled or arrested, he had marched to his girlfriend Eleanor's grade 10 class, pushed the door open and, before the teacher could finish her sentence, said: "I'm leaving, Eleanor. Are you coming or not?" Eleanor put her pen down, walked cool as a cucumber to the back of the class to get her coat, and eloped with Ed in his old Ford. I'm not sure if they even went home first. They drove east for a couple of hours, past the end of the valley and into the mountains, and at a town optimistically named Hope they were married. A few days later, Ed got a job nearby with a crew laying a gas pipeline — it was there that he learned how to operate heavy equipment. Now, maybe 30 years later — he didn't go into detail about the dates, either — they were grandparents.

Finally he said it was quittin' time for him, anyway, and pointing to his pickup, said: "Hop in — let's go look at it now." We drove back down the road and, in the fading light, squelched around the back field. With what was obviously a practised eye, he surveyed the field, agreed that the pond ought to go where it wanted to go, indicated where a ditch should go to drain the pond's overflow, and showed where other ditch lines and drain lines would have to be dug to pick up water from the other fields. Having read Mr. Rennie's 1916 opus, I knew enough to nod authoritatively at the appropriate points and, besides, what Ed said made sense. We agreed on an hourly rate, and he guessed at a total, so, taking a deep breath, I shook hands with him and bade him good evening. Over his shoulder, as he climbed into his pickup, he said he would be able to start in a day or two.

Sure enough, at 5:30 in the morning a couple of days thence, he arrived with his huge machine. On the first day, he dug most of the pond in a shape rather like a boomerang, perhaps in Christine's honour, the curve nestled snugly into the pasture; in the middle, he went down about three metres deep and banked the dug-out earth against the low side to create a knoll. On the second day, he dug a long trench down one side of the property and cut through a blackberry thicket to tie into the township's ditch that ran along the road. On the third day, he dug another ditch down the other side, as well as trenches about a metre deep connecting parts of the fields to the pond and the ditches. And on the fourth day, he laid perforated plastic drain pipe called Big-O in all the trenches and then covered them back over. On the fifth day, he rested. It was two days short of being biblical.

Compared with our neighbour's carefully tended pasture, which looked dry and lush in spite of the wet spring, ours looked like a First World War battlefield, with the tread marks from Ed's tank everywhere. With the amount of clay in the soil it would stay like a gumbo, reminiscent of pottery classes in school, until the spring sun really got at it. In parting Ed had said:

"If the weather ever gets better, come by and borrow my tractor and you can smooth out some of the lumps I've left." The inference was to wait until May, when cultivating the clods of soil would break them down into a fine tilth. In the meantime, though, the pond was filling rapidly.

That first season the pond was clear and pure. The frogs, disrupted by the digging, had quickly moved back and established themselves along the edge; they must have sent word to their distant relatives, because soon there were hundreds of them, all carrying their little suitcases, marching across the fields to our place. At night the air was alive with their ribbeting. Ducks arrived and overnighted. The swallows from the barn swooped and skimmed the water's surface, hunting for the bugs that swarmed above the cool surface in the evening. And it was a beautiful place to swim, although the edges were still muddy and the bottom was solidifying very slowly.

The pasture dried and became green and lush, but it was lumpy and rough anywhere that Ed's digger had been. "Come then, let your sturdy bullocks turn up the rich soil," wrote Virgil in 37 B.C., so I walked up to Ed's to borrow his tractor, which he called Steve, and his implements. Serf and turf. The main weapon of attack was to be a disc harrow — multiple sets of metal discs like dinner plates pierced through the middle and mounted at an angle to the tractor's line of travel. As the harrow was dragged through the rough soil, it dug and turned numerous shallow furrows. It was slow work, and the light harrow tended to ride too high on the rougher bits of soil, but it did break up the ground a little. Then, referring to Mr. Rennie's book as well as to my 1924 copy of *The New Agriculture,* I hitched to the tractor an old chain harrow that had been abandoned years before in the tall grass, tied a log on top of it to keep it down, and dragged it around over the broken soil. The teeth of the chain harrow broke the soil down further and smoothed it so that it was less like moose pasture and more like a farm field. Anyway, I thought, it should be okay for sheep.

33

The big question was whether the grass that was now growing furiously on the field was good fodder or merely pretty green stuff. Lodged in my brain was somebody's comment that all the research money in North America went into turf for lawns and golf courses and that very little went into pasture for animal fodder. On a visit to the local co-op, my eye had been drawn to the bins of grass seed: there was a highlands pasture mix, a lowlands pasture mix, an orchard mix, and several turf mixes; the turf was mainly a creeping fescue, which didn't sound terribly appetizing, even to me, but the fodder grasses were perennial rye, orchard grass, Kentucky bluegrass, timothy, and a number of others in different combinations. What would sheep make of our grass? It seemed unlikely, but I imagined they might waste away in the midst of seeming plenty, while neighbours gathered along our perimeter fences and pointed and laughed.

As I was considering the next step, Christine met Jan through a garden club. He was interested in some of the heritage rosebushes she was growing and came to look at them. Being a country man, that meant a chat, too. He talked about growing up on a farm in Holland but, after the war, with no chance of inheriting or buying enough land to make a living, he had gone into the army and then immigrated to Canada. A man of about 70, or maybe 60, he was medium height and very solidly built after a lifetime of farming and working as a stonemason. He commented in passing that he raised sheep and that the shed on the side of our barn would be an excellent sheep pen.

"Shouldn't sheep go in the barn?" I asked.

"No, they don't get cold, and they need good air circulation," he replied. "Sheep in closed barns around here tend to get pneumonia in winter."

"Oh."

I asked him if he would have a look at the pasture. Out we went through the gate behind the house into what had become a riot of different-coloured grassy panicles and seed heads. Jan gestured at an area about the size of a suburban lot that was dominated by a grass with a pretty purplish-red seed head. "That's redtop," he said. "Sheep will only eat that when it's really young." Another one that I had thought was very attractive and robust turned out to be Yorkshire Fog, the name coming from a Norse word meaning "rank winter grass." However, he identified some clumps of ryegrass and orchard grass and timothy and was pleased with most of what he saw, especially all the native clover coming up on the areas disturbed by Ed's machine. That was an indication of good soil.

As we walked back to the house, he talked a little about farming in Holland before the war. "My father had a saying," he said, "'there are more poor farmers than there is poor land.' I've always believed that."

Oh, great, I thought. It's a variation on the saying "a bad carpenter blames his tools," which I had used throughout my life to justify my lack of skill as a builder. So, if I got animals and they did poorly, I couldn't blame the land.

"Do you think I should get some sheep here?" I asked him.

"Oh," he said, with a twinkle in his eye, "I can't tell you what to do on your own place."

The Pullet Surprise

⟨+ +⟩

Poultry may be managed more successfully than any other farm animal by women and children.
— Henry Jackson Waters, *The New Agriculture,* 1924

CHRISTINE WAS THE POULTRY EXPERT. Twenty years earlier, she had been the caretaker of a National Trust property in Tasmania, an old estate in the countryside where her major function was to report any suspicious activities; for her diligence she received $35 a week and a possum-infested dairyman's cottage as an abode. A neighbour had given her four hens, which she dubbed Whitey, Blacky, Spotty, and Bloody to reflect their pecking order; they had lived and scratched about within the high fence of an abandoned grass tennis court, the only available protection from the foxes that had been imported into Tasmania to provide sport for the "squattocracy" of colonial times. After a year, she had left the cottage and her chickens behind and had moved on. It wasn't much experience, but she *had* had chickens. As in the old saying: "In the land of the blind, the man with one eye is king."

Scanning through the local paper in the "Livestock for Sale" section, she spotted an ad for pullets of a type called the Isa Brown hybrid, ready to lay, for $7 apiece. We thought Isa to be a rather pretty name for a hen and understood them to lay brown eggs, which seemed more natural and organic than the white ones typical of supermarkets and Styrofoam cartons. Accordingly, with a cardboard box in the back of the pickup truck, we motored first to the feed dealer at the nearby town to buy some bags of layer pellets, as the chicken feed was called, and then proceeded o'er hill and dale to Windy Acres Poultry Farms (although there turned out only to be one of it, it was still called a "farms"). To our surprise, we could see no vast throngs of chickens milling about in the spring sunshine, but only a house, a yard patrolled by a particularly nasty Rottweiler, and a metal-clad, windowless building, perhaps 20 metres by 50 metres, with a gabled roof. Piles of what looked like sawdust and chicken manure had evidently been pushed by a tractor out the double doors on one side into a yard, and nearby was a stainless-steel hopper, about the size of a van tipped on end, emblazoned with the slogan CHORE TIME and the logo of a feed company.

I had shut the engine off and was still wondering how I could get to the front door without being eaten by the dog, when out came a middle-aged woman wearing an old padded jacket and gum boots. She called the dog over, ordered it to stay, and marched up to us, asking brusquely: "What can I do you for?"

"Ah, your ad in the paper ... we want to buy some chickens."

"How many?"

"Ah, four!"

"Follow me," she said, and strode off toward the large building.

The outer door led to a small anteroom with another door, which she opened onto a multitude of identical, rusty-brown pullets, their little combs and wattles a pale red colour, all standing around shoulder-to-shoulder on the sawdust floor. It was gloomy dark after the bright sunshine outside, the only light coming from a couple of dim, greenish fluorescent fixtures high above. A couple of large ceiling fans turned lazily, venting the heady ammonia fog from the manure to the outside. While we were taking in the scene, which could have been a chicken's version of Dante's Inferno, the owner plunged into the throng and, to a chorus of squawking, emerged seconds later with two chickens, each hanging by a single leg, in each hand. She stuffed them unceremoniously into our cardboard box, took our money, and bade us farewell.

As we chugged home, keeping an eye on the box in the back of the truck, half expecting it to grow eight legs through holes pecked in the bottom and make a run for it, we compared Windy Acres' operation with what we had read in books and articles about the poultry business. There was no sign of a hatchery, so the operators probably bought day-old chicks, raised them to pullets, and sold them to all the two-bit farmers like us in the valley; all the chickens must have been able to get jobs as there were no nesting boxes visible in the gloom around the perimeter of their building; the light level was kept low to reduce the chickens' desire to wage war and to lower their activity level so they would grow faster; they were floor-raised birds, according to the jargon, with no perch to roost on. "Did you notice they were all debeaked?" Christine asked.

I hadn't, but when we got our quartet home to their new coop and hauled them out of the box, that was the first thing I saw — the points of their beaks had been clipped off to reduce the amount of damage they could do to each other while they sorted out the pecking order in their gulag. Their food had been layer pellets and mash, easy to shovel up with a square beak, and there were, after all, no little seeds or bugs to be seized with an accurate peck. But except for this mutilation, they were beautiful birds, lushly feathered in russet and orange, and stared back at us suspiciously with their glinting, reptilian eyes. They seemed small for full-size chickens, but our reading had told us that the modern layer hen was a compact little soul, bred to convert feed efficiently into eggs without putting too much meat onto herself. I picked one up and felt her breastbone, which was sharp enough to cut cheese. This hybrid was not an eating chicken.

For several days they remained captives, checking out the great outdoors through the wire mesh around the little run attached to their coop. Because real birds don't sleep on the floor, I went down to the coop every evening and lifted each one carefully onto the perch, a piece of dowelling a half-metre above the floor; unfamiliar with the concept of balance, they swayed and flapped a little, occasionally falling to the floor with a thud, but after a few days they had the hang of it and flew up onto the perch themselves. Sundown put them into a docile sleep, and as they perched with their feathers fluffed up against the nighttime cold they crooned little chicken songs to accompany their dreams. Poor chickens, I thought, to have to be taught life skills by one of Plato's "featherless bipeds."

One sunny morn, a few hours after I opened their outside door, the first of them emerged and began the characteristic hunt and peck now usually thought of as a keyboard technique. The others soon followed and, although it was their first time on real earth, they were instinctively chickenlike — as they ranged freely, nothing escaped their sharp eyes, whether bug or fresh blade of grass. By the afternoon, full of bugs and bits, they had found a pile of sun-warmed dirt, dug a hole, and were dust-bathing gleefully — lounging on their sides, eyes closed, and scratching dirt up under their feathers to rid themselves of lice. In their ecstasy, they crooned and chirped a little, and occasionally ate a pebble. After 15 minutes or so, a hen would get up and, with feathers fluffed, shake like a dog, sending a small cloud of dust away on the breeze. Then, taking a long step away from the dust bath, she would resume her search for treats.

A month or so later, by which time we guessed they were about seven months old, they began to lay eggs with firm, bright orange yolks — the classic free-range egg of high-priced specialty stores. They were unfertilized, of course, what the ancient Greeks called *hypenemia oa* or wind eggs, from the belief that the hens were fertilized by the moist south wind. Usually with a great noisy cackling, they laid their eggs in the straw-filled nesting boxes in their coop, almost an egg a day each. Even though they spent their time wan-

dering around the barnyard eating, they always left room for
human food – ancient leftovers, curdled cream, pasta, sour milk,
yoghurt with green fur on top of it, vegetables the consistency of
a cream puff, crumbs from the tabletop, and scraps of meat, *especially chicken,* were all pounced upon enthusiastically and given back
as eggs and manure. At night they were smart enough to go home
by themselves, putting them on a level above most teenagers. All I
had to do was close the door into the run to protect them.

Unlike the chickens of Christine's Tasmanian past, the Isa
Browns didn't develop enough of a pecking order to turn one of
them into a Bloody. The debeaking helped, of course, but they
also had a lot of freedom and space to move in and so, like the
Marlboro Man, were content with their lot in life. From time to
time we added chickens to our little flock, and sometimes sub-
tracted them, which prompted a reshuffling of their pecking order
– the discovery of Norwegian psychologist T. Schjelderup-Ebbe,

who knew chickens to be great guinea pigs. For a time they could get into the garden, where they were attracted to any digging, sometimes even hopping onto the shovel if they saw a worm, but their indiscriminate weeding quickly led to a massive fence-improvement campaign. Soon they were confined to the barnyard and the fields — translated, we were confined to the house and the garden, prisoners of the chickens.

Hens left the flock for a number of reasons. First there were predators, most formidably raccoons, there being no foxes in our part of the world. Unlike dogs, which are well fed and kill for the thrill, a raccoon truly makes a meal out of a chicken, eating everything but beak, feet, feathers, and squawk, as did the occasional coyote that dug under the perimeter fence and nailed a chicken out for an afternoon stroll. Every time we thought our fencing was good, and believed the coop and run to be impregnable, some bright bulb would prove us wrong. On a farm, you only know when your fences are *in*adequate. But these predators were always just passing through, finding house cats and poodles elsewhere to be easier pickings, and they never did such systematic carnage that we and the chickens could not coexist with them. Touch wood, but a dog has never gotten in.

However, I could not coexist with any hen that ate its own eggs. Unless I intervened, everybody would want to try it. So one day, when I walked into the coop and discovered a hen named Yum Yum with egg on her face, I was forced to act. (The first chickens had quite definable personalities and were novelties to us, so they got names: a flighty, rather insincere hen was named Yum Yum after the bride in Gilbert and Sullivan's *The Mikado*; a deep-voiced one with a singsong cackle became Patsy Cline; a Black Orpington that never developed a proper red comb and wattles, and looked like a Victorian granny, became Maiden Auntie, and so on.) So I sharpened the hatchet and went to grab Yum Yum. Hung upside down by her feet, she was calmer than I was, and I thought as I swung her head onto the chopping block, This is going to hurt me more than it will you. But I was wrong. It didn't bother me, and she made good soup. Perhaps she should have been named Anne Boleyn.

As the months went by, I became adept at weeding out the malcontents, and the occasional hen who became seriously sick or egg-bound, and dispatching them quickly at night when they were dormant. In the early times with the flock, our actions usually reflected the folk saying: "When an old Jew [or Russian, or Irishman] kills a chicken, one of them is sick." But it became evident that the Isas, and some of the other odd hybrid birds we had picked up here and there, were good for egg laying but not for much else. They had been bred to lay heroically, almost daily, for the first year, and after that they were all used up and laid very little. For commercial producers this was probably a good stratagem, as every year the old ones could be sold for pet food and new ones brought in; under this system the hens were more a crop than a flock and were nothing but an adjunct to the commercial process of egg production. As Samuel Butler quipped, a hen is only an egg's way of making another egg.

Commercial pressures in the last century have led to this industrialization of the chicken. On the traditional farm, chickens were usually just a part of the barnyard — according to a 1910 census, 80 percent of the 5.5 million American farms kept chickens, an average of 80 each. Chickens, at least hens, were also common in cities and towns: in 1906 there was apparently one chicken for every two North American city-dwellers. For obvious reasons, urban roosters were rare, although in the ancient world only the Sybarites, who hated all noise and disruption, refused to allow roosters into their city.

The chicken species perpetuated itself because a hen in a flock supervised by a rooster laid a dozen or so eggs and then went broody — she sat on the eggs for 21 days, hatched her chicks, and then raised them with the help of a little grain and the household scraps. This usually happened in the spring, when scratch was plentiful, and as time went by the female chicks became pullets and then hens, while the males became cockerels and grew to a fryer size in four or five months. The only roasters were capons — castrated cockerels — that grew plump and juicy partly because they wasted little time and energy in crowing, fighting, and fornicating.

Thus, the eating chicken was traditionally a spring chicken, a seasonal treat, and until the 1950s chicken was more expensive than beef, making the U.S. Republican Party's 1928 campaign slogan of A CHICKEN IN EVERY POT somewhat more deluxe than it seems today. Most farm families sold their spring chickens for cash and ate stewing birds, the old hens and roosters that weren't doing their jobs anymore. Hence the popularity of classic country recipes like coq au vin that render delectable an old bird with the consistency of a boot.

Although the ancient Egyptians had mastered the technology of large-scale incubation, for subsequent millennia most societies were content to let hens hatch the chicks. Many Victorians, for example, even felt that the chicken lifestyle reflected their own values: the Reverend Edmund Saul Dixon, in his 1849 opus on poultry, saw the attentive and lordly rooster as the defender of the female and the keeper of order, while the hen was plump and motherly, busying herself with her children and never intruding into her husband's world. But other Victorians were more scientific and inquisitive, and carefully scrutinized the chicken; among the inventions of that creative age was a gas-fired incubator.

A Danish farmer named Christopher Nisson, who had moved in the 1880s to the agricultural town of Petaluma near San Francisco, did not share Dixon's tolerance of the typical chicken lifestyle. It annoyed him that his hens wasted their time and his by laying their eggs in secret little nests around the barnyard, then disappearing and going broody, then raising their own chicks and not producing eggs for a significant part of the warm months of the year. Hens lay copiously in the spring and, if they are not interrupted by motherhood, keep it up through the summer and fall before moulting, then are

44

effectively on strike until the light level begins to increase as spring approaches. Nisson felt he could manage egg and chick production better than the hens and stockpile eggs for the winter months when they commanded the highest price; he set about improving the best of the newly invented incubators.

He rationalized his egg operation by confining his hens and culling any that defiantly went broody. In search of further efficiencies, he focused on the White Leghorn chicken, a small Italian bird of industrious disposition that laid fashionably white eggs and had less tendency to go broody than such old-fashioned farm chickens as Rhode Island Reds, Barred Plymouth Rocks, and Buff Orpingtons — the dual-purpose birds long popular on North American farms because they were both good egg layers and big enough to eat. At the same time as electric light became available, poultry farmers discovered that artificial light stimulated the hen's pituitary gland and kept her laying through the winter. Nisson's careful breeding, selecting, and management turned poultry, which had once been almost a sideline of farm life, into a specialized industry and made Petaluma "the egg basket of the world." Breeding operations became big business and refined the White Leghorn and other suitable candidates into super chickens: one breeder was the Institut de Sélection Animale in France, which gave its name to our first chickens, the I.S.A. Browns.

Ironically, perhaps, the standardization of the white supermarket egg has created a market for a different egg: free-range for the taste, organic for the food quality, and brown-shelled just because it *looks* more natural (Rhode Islanders bucked the national trend to white eggs a century ago and stuck with their Rhode Island Reds — only then were they certain that their eggs were fresh). There is also a market for free-range chicken, which commands a high price in the specialty stores in the city. A number of traditional chicken breeds could do both jobs, and we soon found that a local hatchery had, in addition to a selection of the modern hybrids, some of the old breeds. After some debate, we settled on Barred Plymouth Rocks, a handsome black-and-white striped, rather plump chicken, one of which, according to Henry Jackson Waters, was the world-champion egg layer of 1924 (324 eggs in the first year of production at the Oregon Agricultural College Experiment Station, in case the question comes up in a trivia quiz).

Near the barn was a low wooden building probably built as a rabbit hutch about 50 years ago. Inside it I strung up an infrared lamp, put out waterers, and scattered some crumbled chick food onto the straw and sawdust on the floor. After a visit to the hatchery on an early summer day, I came away the proud owner of two dozen peeping, dark brown chicks, which returned with me to the new nursery in a straw-lined box about big enough for a pair of children's shoes. I lifted each fragile little bundle of bone and fluff out of the box, dipped its beak carefully into the waterer, and put it on the floor. Right away it began to scratch and peck for food.

They huddled together beneath the lamp when they were cold, ranged about the floor once they had warmed up, scratched in the sawdust, pecked at bits of feed, filled their sharp beaks in the watering trough and tipped their heads back to swallow, and, after a few days, slowly began to grow black-and-white striped feathers in place of their downy birthday suits. I watched them a lot, partly because I was worried they needed a mother and wouldn't know where to turn for advice, but as it turned out they were busy, healthy little souls, hatched with enough information preprogrammed to turn them into successful chickens.

As they feathered out and grew, I was able to raise the infrared light higher from the floor and, after three weeks, remove it altogether. I had bought them unsexed — a mixture of boys and girls just as they had hatched — because we wanted to pick the likeliest male candidate to be our rooster and consign the rest to the pot. Soon they emerged from the old hutch into their fenced run, the little cockerels distinctive with their fledgling fancy tail feathers and their swaggering manner, sometimes squaring off against each other with fluffed-out hackles while the little pullets quietly went about their business. At about five months the cockerels' hormones really kicked in and their run became like a scene from a Billy Jack movie – like the visit of a motorcycle gang to a quiet town. There had turned out to be 10 cockerels and 14 pullets: terribly unfair odds, as the pullets were constantly grabbed and raped (with chickens, there's no question of consent, and they don't pair off like geese or ducks). And the crowing was deafening. It was time to choose who was to be the lucky boy.

At first we thought we would pick the biggest one, and there was a contender – a square, purposeful bird who made a noise as if he had hoovered up a baggie as he strutted around the yard. But after some reflection, we realized he might try to beat us up, too, and so resolved to pick an average one. An overly aggressive rooster could make life miserable around the barnyard, especially after his spurs grew to their full length in a year or so.

One October morning, we got up while it was still pitch-black and went with a flashlight into their house, swiftly picked all but one of the roosters off the perch, made sure the big bruiser was among them, and dispatched them. When the surviving one emerged at dawn, he looked around in a rather stunned fashion and, realizing that somehow he had vanquished all his rivals, he puffed himself up and crowed and crowed. It was time, he seemed to say, to take charge. The following night, we moved them all down into the main henhouse where, after some initial pushing and shoving with the old hens, everyone settled in. A number of them preferred to sleep on the rafters, as high above the floor as they could get, and ascended there in stages, first flying to the perch, then across the coop to the top of the nesting boxes, and then vertically to the rafter nearest the door; from there they hopped across to a favourite spot to sleep. But they flew directly down, with all the aerodynamics of an anvil, when it was time to go out to greet the morn.

47

With all the new chickens, the barnyard took on a different character. The rooster, by now named Arthur, was a slave to his lust: sometimes he did a little dance, chortling in a low and no doubt sexy voice, before seizing a hen by the nape of the neck and mounting her, flattening her into the ground for a few seconds; other times, without warning, he would jump one who just happened to be walking by. Regardless, the object of his desire would, with a little shake to rearrange her feathers, pick herself up, dust herself off, and start all over again, to paraphrase the Jerome Kern song.

Arthur quickly became the centre of their little world and could usually be found in the barnyard or at the compost pile with several hens. If there was any danger about, such as a hawk high in the sky, or if someone came upon them suddenly, he would let out a low, distinctive warning, a pok-POK-p-p-p-pok, with the second note higher-pitched than the others, that put everyone on alert. When a hen was laying an egg, she usually signalled her triumph with the classic chicken cackle — pok-pok-pok-pok-PO-KAAAAAK!-pok-pok-pok-pok (repeated many times) — which Arthur would accompany, if he were anywhere nearby, with the same cackle, except with his deeper voice it sounded like a hen yelling into a kazoo. And, of course, he crowed at dawn, whenever he flew up onto a fence or climbed to the top of the dung heap, or after a particularly satisfying fornication. If two hens started to fight, he would jump between them and, with his beautiful neck feathers standing proud like a knight's chain mail, challenge whichever was the most aggressive. No one ever took him up on it. As Reverend Dixon noted, hens without a rooster were like soldiers without a general: "There is nobody to stop their mutual bickering, and inspire an emulation to please and be pleased."

As entertaining as all of this was, it was incomplete, as no hen had gone broody and hatched a clutch of chicks. It seemed likely that their mothering instinct had been unlearned by generations of hatchery hatchings, and they certainly had had no mother other

49

than the heat lamp. Eventually, though, a switch clicked in one of the hens, who signalled her broodiness by her puffed-up attitude atop some eggs in one of the nesting boxes one afternoon when I was doing the rounds. Good, I thought, but then I realized that it was September, not April.

A few days later when she was truly asleep, I carefully moved her and her eggs to a former dog kennel close to the house. Undisturbed, she continued to sit, and a couple of weeks later hatched a half-dozen chicks — the same peeping little dark brown fluffy balls with beaks that I had started with a year before. Although she had attended no prenatal classes, she was nevertheless a good mother, scratching up little bugs for the chicks, sometimes finding a particular morsel and placing it on the ground in front of one, clucking to them in a tone unlike any she had used when she was just a normal hen, and always lifting her wings and gathering the chicks under her ample skirts whenever they became cold. At night she was quiet like a cottage, with the chicks warm beneath her roof.

But it *was* autumn, and by November there was steady rain, turning the kennel into a muddy mess. So in the middle of the night, down they all went to the main henhouse. In my ignorance, I thought the hen would stay with her chicks but, in the morning when she saw the other hens, she said, "Hey, I'm a chicken, too!" and abandoned her brood. Her mothering instincts only went so far. Fortunately the chicks were well feathered and didn't freeze to death.

In spite of their truncated childhood, the new chicks seemed to be a smarter group than the hatchery ones of their mother's generation. We watched the way they foraged, how they remembered the route to the hole in the fence that got them into the vegetable garden, and how interested the pullets were in sitting eggs. The following spring, the original mother hen went broody again and hatched a few more, which she stayed with protectively till they were well grown. As the generations progressed, we hoped they would unbreed themselves back to the cunning of the chickens of yore. All we wanted was a self-sustaining flock that would supply us with eggs and meat in return for food and protection: mutual dependence, not a bad bargain in these troubled times.

Ewe Haul

⟨+ +⟩

To the dales resort, where shepherds rich,
And fruitful flocks, be everywhere to see . . .
— Edmund Spenser, *The Shepheardes Calender,* 1579

OUR NEIGHBOUR, Angela, had sheep. In the morning, she opened
the gate to a pen near her barn and they filed out — single file, with
no pushing or shoving — walked along a pathway between two lines
of fence, and passed through a Y-shaped gate that opened one pasture and closed off another. She followed after them and closed the
gate to the field. A watering trough stood nearby. In the evening,
the sheep lined up waiting to be let back in. They appeared to have
their own tram track, like office workers content with their regular
employment and routine. Keeping sheep looked easy.

For us the alternatives to sheep were either to buy a big mower
or to have cattle. Jan's review of the grasses had made it pretty clear
that the field would need some plowing and reseeding before it
became good pasture, which meant that it wasn't worth haying to
sell. Besides, the fields were a bit small and irregularly shaped for
modern haying equipment (while there are always farmers willing to
do contract haying, sometimes for a portion of the crop, on fields
like ours they would want cash and would nevertheless be busy on
their own fields during the best haying weather). As for cattle, a
number of people nearby had their fields mowed by beeves —
weaned, castrated steers, usually brown-and-white Herefords with

53

noses like huge pink erasers — that were bought at the country auction and carted around by a character in the livestock hauling business named Ub Iwerks. It seemed a simple way to make a little money, requiring only a block of salt and an automatic watering trough to get into business. But the more I thought about cattle the less I liked the idea: some of our fences seemed feeble, and the beeves were only resident long enough to put on some weight before being picked up again by Ub for the trip to the feedlot for "finishing" or to the abattoir. It didn't seem to be enough like farming for our romantic souls and, besides, Christine had decided she didn't want any animals that were bigger than she was. (Much later she wished she had used the word *heavier,* but that's another story.)

We had contemplated goats, too, but they had a few strikes against them: they were expensive to buy (about $600 each, according to ads in the paper); the only commerce around them was a limited market for their meat, unless you were prepared to milk them incessantly; they were rumoured to leap tall fences with a single bound and devour rose gardens; and the billy goats had horns and a penchant for violence. Which left sheep. Everywhere in rural France we had seen flocks of these picturesque creatures, their bells clanking as they grazed the rough *garrigue*. They seemed gentle and docile and, indeed, our neighbour had them.

Angela and her husband Chuck had the farm to the north, between us and the winery; they were refugees from the city, like us, and were enjoying an early retirement. Chuck thrived on the work of a farm: fencing, moving around piles of earth and manure, and manicuring his pastures with a big tractor and some expensive-looking implements; with the rest of his time he trained quarter horses. Their place was picture-book neat. Every morning they walked the boundaries with an old Labrador dog following closely behind, so one day I went out to the fence to talk to them as they went by.

After the obligatory half hour of country conversation, on everything from other neighbours to politics to the weather, I felt I could cut to the chase. On the matter of maintaining a flock of sheep, Angela was very reassuring: all I really would need at this time of the year was a bucket and a block of salt; good fences helped, as a sheep on the road was an endangered sheep; wintertime was more work, as was lambing, and Chuck chipped in that he didn't like Angela to be in the same field as the ram. Unfortunately they didn't have any ewes for sale, as they had taken several to the auction the previous week, so my timing was just a little off.

"Have you met Jan?" she asked. "He's got really good sheep."

"Romneys," said Chuck. "Good for wool, but the carcass doesn't dress out as big as these Suffolks," he added, pointing at a black-faced, long-eared sheep grazing not far away while keeping a wary eye on the dog.

"The Mitchells there" — Angela gestured in the general direction of a place up the hill — "swear by their Hampshires. Nice, quiet sheep. And big... but the wool's no good... you might as well throw it in the compost as try to sell it."

"Depends on what you want to do," said Chuck. "Now Harry Wright down on Townline Road, he has Dorsets because they lamb pretty well year round. More profit in that."

"Well, uh, I don't know.... I thought it made sense to have some sheep on here," I mumbled, having abandoned my earlier plan to sound knowledgeable and decisive.

"Good idea!" Chuck said. "They keep the place nice and neat. If you want to make money, though, you should get some feeder calves. You could put 'em in that field over there if you fixed the fence."

"Well, I ... uh, there's a lot to be done here.... I want to take it slowly."

"I know...," chipped in Angela. "Call Dave Thompson — he's in the phone book, the Thompson on Brown Road. He'll pay you a little bit to pasture some of his sheep for the summer, and take them back in the fall. That way you can see if you like it."

I thanked them for the advice and let them continue their morning walk. While I trudged back to the house through the lengthening grass, I wondered whether I should plunge right in with permanent sheep or whether I should call this Dave guy. I had meant to ask what a sheep cost. Christine and I had agreed that we would get animals that had other uses than just dinner — the chickens with their eggs fit that bill, but of the sheep Angela and Chuck had mentioned only the Romneys seemed to have an additional asset in their wool. Maybe it would be simplest to give the rent-a-sheep guy a call.

I did, and he returned my call that evening. Sure, he said, how many did I want? Twelve? They were $40 sheep, he said, and he would buy them back for $50 after a couple of months. "Have you got a pen?" he asked. Presuming that he didn't mean the thing you write letters with, I said yes, remembering Jan's comment about the fenced area under the shed roof. He told me to find some kind of

feeding trough, about 12 sheep wide would be perfect, and some kind of water bucket or tub that they couldn't knock over, and then he promised to come by the following afternoon.

I was just finishing nailing together a rough feeder when Dave arrived in a big pickup truck pulling a long metal trailer with the words EWE HAUL painted on the front. Dave was about 70, or maybe 65, a stocky, rather leathery man who moved like 40 and talked 19 to the dozen, as my mother used to say. We shook hands and, well, we talked and talked, and it went something like this: he was a retired school principal but had grown up on a farm just over the next hill; his hobby was buying and selling animals; if anybody needed an old animal taken to the auction, for example, he would do it and charge a small fee; the sheep were from a contractor doing organic maintenance of power-line clearings and were in need of fattening on good grass.

I opened the door into the pen and he backed the trailer up to the edge of it. Out shuffled a dozen rather bony sheep with very short, dirty wool, the most unprepossessing flock I had ever seen. They were obviously agitated and moved rapidly about, quickly exploring into every corner.

"What kind are they?" I asked.

"Oh, they're just junk sheep," Dave replied. "You can see some Cheviot in that one," he said, pointing. "They're good lawn mowers."

I looked back into the trailer and realized that there was an old goat still standing there. "Don't worry about her," Dave said. "I picked her up on the way here. She's got arthritis real bad – she'll go for sausage at the auction...." He laughed. "Don't ever ask what goes into political deals or sausage!"

He left me with a bucket of grain and directions to rattle it if I wanted the sheep to come.

Out they went to the pasture the following morning and roamed everywhere. I mean *everywhere*. Anything other than the sturdiest wire fence could not hold them; they zipped through narrow gaps in old fences, hopped between horizontal boards that had once held cattle, plowed through hedges, and were a complete nuisance. I had thought they would cross the ditches at the crossings, but they were agile and surefooted beyond my wildest imagination – opportunistic sheep, no doubt a result of the conditions of their previous employment. They annoyed me, but I reassured myself that either they or I would settle down.

A week went by, and still they hadn't calmed down. On the Saturday, some friends came from the city for lunch; we sat in the shade of a big maple tree in the yard and looked out at the bucolic scene, marred only by the antsy, nervous, dirty dozen. After one glass of wine too many, someone commented: "Those sheep are really ugly." Dammit he's right, I thought, but put the wine away out of spite, anyway. A couple of days later I called Dave, making the lame excuse that my fences weren't up to his sheep, and asked him to come and take them back. "No problem," he said equably, "I'll dose 'em on grain for a week. I'm trying to put together a hundred for a job up north."

The experience taught me three things: first, to choose my friends more carefully, and second, that the fence had some obvious weak spots. Hoping that Chuck wasn't watching with binoculars, I plugged holes with old bits of wire and stretched a line of fence to a swinging Y-shaped gate; looks like Dogpatch, I thought. The third thing was that if I were to bond with the sheep (in a platonic way, of course), they had to be animals of character and permanent residents.

Jan did not seem surprised by my call. "Your timing's good," he said. "I was just talking with a woman near here who's selling two Seagrave Romney ewes, and I've got a couple I can sell you." We talked for a while (naturally) and I learned some worthwhile things: he raised Romneys, a breed developed on Romney Marsh in Kent, which was lowland pasture with a tendency to be wet, just like our place; a Seagrave was a Romney variation bred for fleece – the life's work of a breeder in Oregon – but Jan's purebred Romney fleeces were just as popular with spinners and weavers and had won "Best Fleece" ribbons in the agricultural shows; you improved your flock by ruthlessly selecting and culling; he wouldn't sell me ewes without also selling me a ram, as ewes "waste away like snow in spring if they're not bred"; he had an old ram called Oscar, "part New Zealander," that we could have; the ewes were $150 apiece and the ram $200; and if I came up tomorrow, we could load them into his truck and bring them down.

After lunch the following day, I drove the half-dozen kilometres to the address he had given me and found another tidy, picturesque property at the end of a dead-end road. In the driveway was a little Mazda truck, about the same size as our ancient Toyota, with wooden sides a metre tall bolted to the bed. I followed him to his open-sided barn and got a tour of his sheep operation. He walked smoothly and quietly among the 30 or so ewes and, using some portable fence panels tied together with baler twine, herded them effortlessly together at one end of the pen. Pointing at two ewes among all the faces, which on first glance all looked the same, he said they were the two for me. He climbed over the fence in among them and, after some pushing, shoving, and dragging, had them at the edge of the little enclosure. I held one and he took the other.

A few minutes of instruction followed. We looked at their teeth (only on the bottom jaw — the top jaw has a hard, fleshy pad) and felt their udders and along their jawlines; with a quick movement (shepherd's judo), he flipped the 60-kilogram animal onto its rump, pulled a jackknife out of his back pocket, and began to trim her cloven hooves. Then it was my turn. After some huffing and puffing and triple the time, I had the second ewe done. He took two halters from a nail on the wall, haltered one ewe and tied her to the gate; then I haltered the second one and we led her, with the amount of shoving familiar to anyone who has seen a sheep in a Christmas pageant, toward the truck. With a heave-ho we lifted her in, and Jan, still holding the end of the halter, climbed up and lashed her to the stanchion attached to one of the wooden sides. We loaded the other ewe and then went to a second pen where a ram, large but reassuringly docile, gazed thoughtfully at the ewes.

The ram came out quite willingly but took more holding. He was very solid, built like a bulldozer, and probably weighed twice what the ewes had, although he stood about the same height — about mid-thigh on me. Jan ran through the inspection procedure, except instead of udders we checked out his enormous testicles, which hung down almost to the ground. "Don't pat him, and don't ever turn your back on him," he said, "especially during breeding season." Finally, with a heroic effort, we got him into the truck, climbed in, and drove off to the second farm.

"I wanted you to see how to buy a sheep," Jan said, referring to the inspection, "and to assure myself they were in good shape." He talked on a bit about buying sheep and how I should have asked if the parents were around. "My father used to say to me, 'When you find a girl you think you want to marry, get yourself invited into the kitchen and have a good look at the mother.'" He chuckled and continued: "It's the same for picking animals – the apple never falls far from the tree."

At the second farm, it took only a minute to load the two ewes, so the five of them stood nose-in like cars parked along the main street of a country town. The two Seagraves had longer, thinner faces than Jan's Romneys and less wool around their eyes and on their legs. The fleece was about half as long as a finger and was lustrous and white – actually it was beige, in the word's original meaning, the colour of unwashed wool, which seemed a suitably yuppie colour for our farm. In another six months, Jan said, they would need to be shorn. "That would be in February," I remarked with my noted mathematical ability. "Won't they get cold?"

Jan told me he believed in winter shearing and advised that they would not suffer if I spread some extra straw around their pen, kept them in for a day or two, and gave them some grain to increase their metabolism. "You'll probably be lambing in March," he said, "and you want to get the fleece off them first. The stress of birth reduces the quality of the fleece, and the lambs love to climb all over their mothers with their shitty feet. And you'll see that lambs love to sleep on top of their mothers on a cold night with all that heat radiating out." He went on to say that ewes with full fleeces, whether they have lambs with them or not, won't readily seek shelter in really bad weather.

In their new digs, the fearless five fitted in much better than had the dirty dozen. Sure, they were...uh, sheepish, but that was to be expected. Slowly they got used to me, and to their pen and the pasture. As they were permanent critters, they needed names: after toying briefly with Bunctious and Alamadingdong for the ram, we settled on Eric — he seemed like an Eric. The two Seagraves became Gladys and Mary, and the two Romneys Norah and Jenny. Along with the names came our interpretation of their personalities, which we were sure we could see reflected in their big brown eyes. A Romney is a really cute sheep — honestly — just about as pretty as a Jersey cow.

Mary quickly became their leader — the bellwether, except of course she wasn't a wether, which I knew from my new fund of knowledge to be a castrated ram. The other sheep followed her in single file when she went out into the pasture and followed her back when she decided it was time to seek the shade. Eric bumbled along behind them, like a husband on a shopping trip. In almost no time, they had cut a neat little path two hooves wide between their pen and the field; after a couple of weeks, I swung the Y-shaped gate the other way, and they cut a path into that pasture, too. Jan had told me to move them around every few weeks and had quoted a Scottish maxim: "Never let the parish bell ring thrice on the same pasture." The grass recovers faster and the sheep ingest fewer intestinal worms when they are moved from pasture to pasture (just like dogs, cats, and horses, sheep need to be wormed). When I wanted them to come in, I rattled a bucket with a little grain: the sound of the grain was magical, an animal Esperanto, the only drawback being it brought all the chickens, too.

The cooler weather of September triggered the ewes' breeding cycle, and a stunning personality change in Eric. He emerged from his shuffling, slumbering summertime torpor and, almost overnight, became an ovine Don Juan, a rammish Valentino. The trigger was a cloud of come-hither perfume enveloping a ewe, who was likely as not motoring along slowly nibbling on the grass. With his dark brown eyes smouldering, Eric would amble up behind, sniff, throw his head back and pull back his top lip in an expression of bozo ecstasy, then shoulder up to the ewe and give her a little shove. "Hey! Wake Up!" he seemed to be saying, like the joke about foreplay. Having spent some time in nightclubs we knew what was going on and, not wanting to be seen as competition, I stayed well out of his way. When a ewe finally came into heat, she would stand still and well braced and, looking rather self-conscious and demure, allow herself to be mounted. Eric, huge and woolly like a bear, his eyes wild and tongue hanging out, earned his keep.

After Arthur's rather cavalier fornication of the hens, we were intrigued by Eric's romancing ways. He and the ewe would stay together for much of the day, sometimes standing head-to-head, sometimes grazing together; he would mount her many times and then, as her scent faded, lose interest and begin to check out the other ewes. After several days he had "settled" them all, as shepherds say, and had lost most of his aggression toward me.

As fall passed slowly into winter, the fields lost their green richness and became golden, then grey in the dull light. The sheep ambled about, nibbling a little here and there, but by three in the afternoon they were waiting at the gate to be let in for feeding. According to Jan, the ideal day for a sheep is about eight hours of grazing beginning at dawn and divided into three periods, and about the same amount of time chewing the cud, with the balance spent sleeping and socializing; winter varied the routine so that they had about six hours of nibbling, an hour of serious hay scarfing, and the balance loafing and cud chewing in their pen. As their fleeces grew out so that they looked like rolled-up shag carpets with a leg at each corner, they spent a lot of time scratching themselves — a chin on the edge of the feeder, a side on one of the roof posts, a bum on a rough spot on the gate. Christmas came and went as usual, although we were disappointed that no one came on a donkey seeking shelter in our stable.

The shearer, a Welshman named Geoff, came early in February on a mild day. We talked until it was nearly dark and then had to string up lights so that he could see what he was doing, but when he talked to the sheep with his Welsh accent they all did as they were told. As each fleece peeled off, we stuffed it into giant-size garbage bags labelled with the name of the sheep. When they were all done, we went inside for coffee and, after I had seen him on his way, I returned to the pen to see how the sheep were doing. I could hardly recognize them — they were like army recruits, pig-shaved to remove their individuality. To keep warm they had burrowed little nests for themselves in the fresh straw.

A few weeks later they had grown a centimetre or so of wool and began to look familiar again. They were all in the last days of their five-month pregnancy, announced by their bulging sides, distended udders and teats, and lumbering gait. Their life focused around the hay feeder. Late in the afternoon, with a cold wind blowing outside, they came in from the stubble pasture and stood with heads almost buried in the hay, filling the pen with the sound of their munching. I plugged in a lamp, which threw a golden light on the golden straw, and at night they lay quietly, rhythmically chewing their cuds, lost in their thoughts of impending motherhood. Will it be a boy *and* a girl, they wondered, as they knew that if they twinned it made them valuable to their ruthless shepherd. Every time I walked down to the pen, I wondered what I would see. Would I be there for the first birth? Would I know if it was going okay? Jan had said to call if I thought anything was wrong.

He had also said that the ram would be a problem as lambing approached. "The ewes emit the same smell as they do in heat," he explained, "and the ram thinks he has to go back to work." Eric signalled his pending fatherhood by shoving at the now-bloated ewes and charging at me — butting the hand that feeds, as it were. So I pushed him into a pen at the other end of the shed where he quickly became more interested in food than sex. We waited and watched. The ewes' udders and teats were supposed to become a bright red within a few hours of lambing — "Is *that* the colour?" we would ask each other.

Finally, on a rainy Saturday evening while we were on our way back from a friend's wedding in the city, Gladys had her lambs. Scarcely wanting to take the time to get out of my suit, I switched on the light and saw her, the afterbirth still hanging out, licking a little wet bundle in the straw; a second lamb had shakily gotten to its feet and was staggering along almost blindly looking for Gladys's teat and baaing a little baby cry, half human, half sheep. Gladys was murmuring, a sound different from any of the sheeps' normal grunts and baas — it was a sound like the hen's soft clucking to her newly hatched chicks. But there was a third, smaller bundle in the straw nearby; its head was up, but it was making no attempt to stand. I opened the gate and went into the pen. The two big lambs were a boy and a girl; the runt in the straw was another girl.

Picking up the two large lambs, still slippery and weak from the birth, one in each hand, and carrying them low to the ground with Gladys following, I moved slowly across the pen toward a lambing enclosure I had nailed and lashed together using a number of portable fence panels like those I had seen at Jan's. Gladys quickly settled into the new pen, continuing to lick one lamb while lifting a back leg to expose a teat for the other. I carried the runt in and put her in with the other two; Gladys licked her for a minute but soon turned her attention back to her two stronger lambs. The other ewes hung around and watched but kept a respectful distance. Mercifully it was night, and the pesky chickens were at home in their coop asleep. The barn cat was away hunting.

Within a half hour or so, both of the strong lambs had found Gladys's teats and drunk their fill of colostrum, the mother's first milk that is so rich in antibodies and nutrition it all but guarantees a lamb's survival. But the runt had not drunk; she had gotten to her feet and made a halfhearted attempt to find the teat only to lie down again. She seemed cold. It was 10 o'clock at night.

We phoned Jan who was as good as his word. Put the coffee on, he said, he would be down in a few minutes. By the time he arrived a wind had blown up and Gladys had lain down to rest in the straw with the two healthy lambs sleeping up against her. Jan had brought a little bottle of a frozen yellowish-white substance, which he said was colostrum. "It's last year's," he explained. "Whenever I get a strong ewe with just a single lamb, I milk out her other side and save it for emergencies." While he warmed a small plastic bottle with a rubber nipple attached to it under the tap, Christine thawed the colostrum in a makeshift double boiler on the stove. Finally all was ready, the warmed colostrum tested for temperature on the inside of Christine's wrist like milk for a baby.

Jan knelt in the straw and cradled the cold little lamb on its rump between his legs; after a minute or two, she began to warm up and let out a tiny cry that caused Gladys to open her eyes and murmur acknowledgement. "C'mon, little fart," Jan said in a low voice, his best approximation of the mother's call. The lamb began to suck on the rubber nipple; she stretched herself up and drank and drank and, in a few minutes, had emptied the bottle. Jan put her in the straw next to the other lambs, got up, and said: "You've got yourself a bottle lamb."

Gladys was already a fairly old ewe and somehow knew she didn't have enough milk for three, so she focused her attention on her two lambs with the best chance of survival. As early as I could the following morning, I went out to get some goat's milk (the closest thing to sheep's milk available) and, with an empty beer bottle from my private collection and the nipple Jan had left, became mum (or at least feeder) to the runt; Gladys did the mothering. For the first few days I fed her every four hours, then, as she grew, every six, and finally every eight. After three days in the enclosure, Gladys and her threesome went out and joined the others grazing in the field. The lambs slept together in a little heap in the grass. Whenever they woke, they began a series of little bleats that would draw a murmuring response from Gladys. The two big ones would promptly run to her, leaving the little one behind, looking a bit stunned and bereft. But as soon as I appeared in the field she would gallop to greet me and drink her bottle dry.

In the meantime, two more ewes had lambed effortlessly, both with twins, leaving us with only one to go. Gritting our teeth in sympathy with the babies, we had docked all their tails, given them shots, and clipped on ear tags. There was only one to go — Jenny, who kept us waiting until the afternoon of a miserably cold St. Patrick's Day, when she didn't come in with the others. Christine let in the mums and lambs while I walked out into the driving sleet. It was hard to see anything at all looking across the two-hectare field, but I finally spotted a likely looking beige lump in a hollow in the grass.

Jenny was down on her side, having delivered one lamb already. She had turned herself around and was licking the helpless, exhausted little thing to try to dry it. Every minute or so, she would push and labour in an attempt to deliver another; protruding from her uterus was a curious yellow bump which, on closer inspection, was the nose, part of the head, and one hoof of a lamb. The birth sac, bright yellow from the amniotic fluid, was stretched tight across the bump like a bank robber's mask. Evidently the lamb was stuck, one leg turned back and the knee locked against Jenny's pelvic bones. From pictures I had seen in sheep books, the standard trouble-free delivery position was nose and both front hoofs together like a springboard diver.

Christine arrived from the barn and knelt down at Jenny's head, cradling it and holding her while I prepared to be James Herriot. After a false start, because I had forgotten to remove my wedding ring, I got a hand in and, massaging slowly the space between the lamb and the uterine wall, made some progress inward toward the pelvic bone. It was not an unpleasant thing to do in the middle of a storm, as everything was very warm and wet. At first I couldn't distinguish one bit from the next, but once I identified the second

67

shoulder it was easy to slide my hand down to the knee locked behind the pelvis. The pressure of my hand caused the poor sheep to labour intensely, and her powerful contractions squeezed my arm in a hot, painful vise. But suddenly the knee popped by and the lamb slipped, steaming, onto the sleet-covered grass. As I wiped the fluid away from its nose, it began to kick and struggle and I placed it closer to Jenny's head so that she could take over. By the time I had turned back, a third lamb was emerging smoothly onto the grass.

Although it would have been nice to let everyone take five and rest, it was getting dark and we had to get them back to the barn. Christine picked up a lamb, I took two, and we started off, bent double like Quasimodo in *The Hunchback of Notre Dame* to keep the lambs near the ground and well within Jenny's field of vision. As the sheep books put it, lambs don't fly, so you have to carry them low.

The barn was an impossibly distant 200 metres away. Jenny heaved herself up, trailing her afterbirth, and lumbered along behind us. An eternity (or maybe only a few minutes) later they were all in the dry enclosure, with the three lambs competing for the mother's two teats.

After that day, the rest of the spring was an anticlimax. We had survived our first obstetrical emergency, as had the lambs. The ewes knew what they were supposed to do. Within a couple of weeks, all the lambs were racing around together in the pasture. The sun had turned warm and the grass lush and green. The ewes pottered about, gaining weight and strength and calling their lambs regularly for feeding. Although the bottle lamb was a friendly little soul, she usually preferred the company of sheep to people, and began at about four weeks to nibble on the grass. I weaned her at six and, although she soon became almost indistinguishable from the others, she would always perk up a little when I came into sight. A distant dinner gong still rang somewhere in her memory.

Farm Pets

⟨+ +⟩

*How many of us have smacked our lips over a juicy young chicken, a fat
goose, a duck done to a turn, or that king of the American barnyard,
whose final throne is our Thanksgiving table — the great bronze turkey?*
— F. G. Carpenter, *How the World Is Fed*, 1907

WE HAD A WAY OF DISTINGUISHING one farm animal from the next.
If it had a name, it was a keeper. If not, it was probably destined for
somebody's dinner table, often because it was a ram lamb or a cock-
erel and we already had the breeding line we wanted. It is the same
thing with vegetables — either you keep the strongest for your seed
or eventually you starve.

In that way, the farm-animal world is very different from much
of the human world: females are in greater demand than males. As
long as she is a good specimen of a desirable breeding line, a female
critter probably has a future, either on your farm or on somebody
else's. However, the 50 percent of births that are male need a different treatment — if kept around till the time when he matures sex-
ually, a boy will fight until he is dominant, dead or, at the very least,
too injured and submissive to earn his keep. Before that point, on
most farms, he gets invited to a barbecue.

This is not to say that a farm cannot have its pets. Usually they're
cats and dogs, and although they might be thought of romantically
as working animals, they probably get a level of care beyond what any
farm beast might expect. We inherited a barn cat that was all but

feral: she used the barn for shelter and kept it as free of rats and mice as she could, but she would have nothing to do with us, even if called with the falsetto "Heeeeeere, kitty-kitty-kitty!!!" that works with every other cat on the planet. According to the previous owners, she had managed to push out the other stray cats and kittens; having tired of the parade of feral toms — four-legged travelling salesmen, as it were — the smell of spray, and the constant birthing of kittens in the barn, they had live-trapped her and whipped her off to the nearby vet for spaying, and advised us that we might have to help her get rid of any particularly large and vicious cats that tried to roust her from her castle. Remembering Edwina Schneider and the kitten-drowning episode, I eagerly complied and decided to feed her a little every night just for loyalty. Although she got a name, Gretchen, she kept her distance, ignoring all overtures of friendship; nevertheless, as the years went by we came to a certain understanding until, at feeding time, she had abandoned her suspicions enough to stand patiently by her bowl, within an inch of my hand. There was no point in petting her and taming her, as the next thing would be her little nose pressed against the house's French door on a cold night, and us in the market for a barn cat.

Dogs were another matter. I wasn't a dog person and felt about them much as I do about humans — I disliked the species but liked some of the individuals. We knew enough about sheep and chickens, on the one hand, and dogs on the other, to be aware that the latter were traditionally the enemy of the former; yes, a dog could be trained and controlled and managed, but it was a rare canine owner who was able to balance that level of management so that a dog wouldn't chase sheep and kill chickens and yet still be a huggable, drooling bowwow for visiting children to play with. Doug's Border collies, on the farm in Australia, were rarely petted, and then only by him, demonstrating an attitude held by most experienced stockmen on the matter of farm dogs. From him and elsewhere we had learned that in the country animals like dogs could not be free — if they were, they became a problem to something or someone else. Most predator crises in "urban-shadow" areas are caused by dogs whose owners believe they are "free spirits." Sheep and chicken farmers have either good fences and guns or else keep the phone number of the local agricultural agent and dogcatcher readily at hand.

"Aren't you going to get a dog?" city friends asked. *"Aren't you worried about people just coming onto your property?"* We agreed that the lack of a watchdog was a bit of a concern and were still pondering what to do when we met a man with a brogue at a party who regaled us with stories about the geese that patrolled the distilleries in Scotland; a lightbulb went off in Christine's head, and when she got home she pulled her childhood copy of Konrad Lorenz's *King Solomon's Ring* out of the bookshelf and read to me about geese. "I saw a sign on the road when I was coming home the other day," she told me. "'Geese for Sale,' it said. We should go by."

We did nothing about it immediately but, as the goose emporium was on the busy road between us and town, inevitably a day came when we were going by with time to spare and made a snap decision to pull over. Waiting until all the non-goose purchasers passed by, I backed up and made the sharp turn into the driveway. A house that would not have been out of place in the nearby suburbs stood at the end; around it on three sides was an expanse of mud, low wire fences held up by sticks, and a few lean-tos not fit for a junkyard dog. In the compounds defined by the fencing there was a great and diverse collection of poultry, all clucking, quacking, and honking. On the fourth side of the house, protected from the rabble, was a well-maintained vegetable garden with strings stretched taut to mark its rows. An elderly woman in a cheap print dress put down her hoe and walked over to us. "Is that you, Edwina?" I muttered to myself.

She was civil but brusque, in the standard country manner — we were strangers after all. As we walked over to survey her flock, we told her that we wanted a mating pair.

71

"I've only got two left for sale. I think they're a pair ... too young to tell," she said. I had the uncomfortable feeling she was sizing us up. "Seven dollars each."

Same price as pullets. Being neophytes at geese, we said in unison: "Ah, okay."

"You gotta go get 'em! I've got a heart condition!" she declaimed. "I'll get you a cardboard box."

"I'm not dressed for this," I thought as I climbed over the wire fence, the birds scattering ahead of me. Some Pekin ducks flapped out of my way, quacking wildly, as I narrowed my chase to the two long-necked white things — God, they were young, still with spiky head feathers like members of a juvenile punk-rock band — that had run into a corner and were screaming like F-18s. I grabbed one — a hand under the body, another on the snakelike neck — and climbed back over the fence toward the waiting cardboard box. Another trip back in and I found the second one backed into the corner and hissing loudly, but its three-kilogram body was no match for me and I soon had it stuffed into the box with its mate. We paid and were gone.

On the drive back, Christine pointed out that my shirt was streaked with goose shit — "Oh, and your pants, too," she added helpfully — and asked whether I had noticed the other geese there. I had been too focused on the dynamic duo, I told her. Why?

"I wonder if she's sold us a couple of duds."

"How can you have dud geese?" I asked.

Back at the ranch, the twosome settled in happily, hissed and honked at anything that moved (making them about as valuable as the average guard dog), and soon lost their punk haircuts. They were snow-white with orange bills and feet and had the brightest, clearest cobalt-blue eyes; they were Embdens, Dutch farm geese, a little more upright than the brown-and-grey Toulouse geese (or Screwloose geese) we had seen on French farms (not to mention in restaurants as pâté de foie gras and confit d'oie.) Their mannerisms were charming: sometimes they stood on one leg and stretched the

73

other behind in a parody of an arabesque, other times they rushed around with outspread wings like the corps de ballet in *Swan Lake*; they bathed and groomed often and elegantly, dipping their heads gracefully into the water and pulling them up with their chins tucked in, making the most of the plastic wading pool we had provided for them or any convenient puddle or ditch after a rainstorm. Saint-Saëns could have provided the appropriate musical accompaniment when they were in their reflective, self-absorbed mood; Wagner would have suited them the rest of the time. At night we herded them into the old dog kennel, renamed the Little Goose Coop, but during the day they were free to patrol, which they did decorously like sentries, never getting more than a few steps apart. No one could get anywhere near the place without us knowing about it, so they earned their keep. However, as neither of us particularly wanted to eat goose, they had to be pets.

But which was which? When we were at the local co-op buying feed, we took the opportunity to read the goose-sexing section of a book on poultry management. "Restrain the young goose," it said, "insert the finger into the anus and move it around in a circular manner several times. The sexual organs appear when pressure is then applied along the sides of the vent." Snickering like schoolboys at the adult magazine counter in a drugstore, and turning heads all over the store, we retreated. So that's where the term *goosing* came from. We decided to let them figure it out for themselves.

But how to name such silly geese? We were drawn irresistibly to the English aristocracy, where traditionally many names were interchangeably boy/girl: Vivian, Evelyn, Jocelyn, and so on. In fairness, there were also modern names that would have done for either: Leslie, Laurie, or Ronnie, for example. Being tradition-minded people, we settled for Hilary and Beverley; Hilary was slightly smaller and had a small black mark below the right eye. As they grew, he/she demonstrated more aggression. We picked him for the male.

He certainly behaved like one. As spring advanced, he wooed

74

Bev persuasively and clambered onto her, assuming the distinctive wings-down, thrusting position familiar to art connoisseurs from Leda and the Swan paintings. The next thing we knew there was a pile of eggs in some old hay at the back of the barn and a very aggressive, hissing goose atop them. First it was Bev. Then: "Hey, was that Hilary sitting the eggs?" It seemed unlikely that they would share parenting duties like nineties couples, but.... Anyway, a month later all the eggs had cracked or rotted and nothing had hatched. We put it down to inexperience: Lorenz had noted that some breeds of gander have to reach the age of three before they can successfully mate.

As they grew up, they became inseparable, like Tweedledum and Tweedledee. Compared with the other animals, they were very sociable and at their happiest when allowed into the garden while Christine was weeding. On summer afternoons they sat motionless together like plastic lawn swans; when they thought they deserved some attention, they became mischievous and drank from water buckets or got too close to little plants. Usually they could be placated with a dandelion each, which they consumed root and all with a loud, garbled honking noise.

The year passed and spring came around again. Lust was in the air in the farmyard, and the odd couple spent many happy times together grooming and copulating in the little plastic wading pool. Because Bev was nosing around the back of the barn in a dark corner, I threw in a small pile of hay and the following morning found an egg. The next day there was Hilary, in another corner, guarding another egg. They sat on their separate clutches for a month and emerged pale and mournful when nothing hatched. Gay geese. Christine composed an advertisement for the local paper: "Two white geese seek similar male for long-term relationship, perhaps children." We await the response.

✦

WE HAD ALSO INTENDED to get ducks, specifically for their reputation as devourers of slugs. We had lots of slugs, especially in wet years, and one day during a conversation over too much wine with Joyce, an eccentric friend from the city, the subject turned to slug control. There was the stomping method, the snipping method (using pruning shears), the stale beer method, and the slug-bait method. Slug bait is not organic, and beer was never allowed to go stale at our place; stomping and snipping were useful, but it was difficult to be systematic about it without eventually tossing the proverbial cookies.

"Ducks are good — they're little carnivores," I noted.

"We should do a rent-a-duck service for city gardens," said Joyce. "Organic slug control."

"Slugbusters!"

"Yeah."

"And an organic lawn-mowing and fertilizing service, using the sheep," I declared, warming to the subject.

As you can tell, the conversation was going nowhere, and we soon left that topic for another. But a month or so later Joyce called and said she needed help. She explained that she had been part of the committee putting together a charity auction to benefit the university's botanical garden and had had the great idea of auctioning a couple of farm ducks as organic slug controllers.

"Sounds good," I said. "When's this going to happen?"

"Last week — I've already sold them. Woman from a nursery bid $100 for them."

"Great!" I said. "Where'd you get them from?"

"That's why I'm calling you," she said. "You told me about the people down the road having ducks, and I thought you might be able to buy a pair from them and, if not, maybe you know someone else...."

"When do you need them?" I asked.

"I've got to deliver them on Saturday."

"Oh."

"Sorry," she said. I told her I would do what I could.

Fortunately the neighbours down the road were downsizing their duck flock and were willing to part with a pair as long as I promised — I mean, *promised* — not to give them to anybody who would eat them. I swore to protect them forever, and on Saturday morning I strapped an old dog carrier to the bucket on the tractor and chugged down the road to get them. They were a beautiful pair — the duck a sleek Cayuga with black feathering that had a green sheen to it when the light caught it a certain way; the drake a Khaki Campbell, tall and distinguished in shades of brown and olive green like a Harris tweed. They were classic farm ducks, unable to fly more than a few feet at a time, but happy waddling around the barnyard or swimming in a pond. As I chugged back home I thought, These should be for us.

Joyce arrived from the city sounding very apologetic. "I called the nursery people and said I was going to bring over their ducks," she said. "They just laughed. 'Oh, my dear! We couldn't *possibly* have ducks here — it was just a donation.... Goodbye!' Click."

"Oh well, I guess they can live here," I mock-grumbled. "It's not really a problem."

We decided to let them out of the cage. The duck emerged first, then the male. Both looked uncertain. Suddenly, out of the corners of our respective eyes, we all noticed a frog hopping past. Before any of us could exclaim, "Oh, look at the cute little frog!" the duck had raced over and gobbled it up! Then, self-possessed and businesslike, she collected her mate and led him off for a tour of the environs. Before long they had discovered the plastic goose pond and had a swim and a preen. The geese and chickens didn't pay them any attention, and Gretchen calmly surveyed the scene from atop some bales of hay just inside the barn door. If nothing else, these ducks were adaptable.

Like the geese, but unlike the chickens, the ducks had a sort of pet quality to them, and so inevitably they were named: Joyce and

Bill. Also like the geese, they were very easy to herd and could be marched off to a particular area of the garden to go to work. No poultry can successfully be led without the famous grain bucket, and chickens can't be herded at all. While we're on the subject, sheep also can't be herded (except by a sheepdog) but are easy to lead, with or without the grain bucket.

Before we became duck owners, I had built a larger compound for the geese, dubbed Fort Goose, having decided that the Little Goose Coop was more useful for hens and chicks. At first we tried putting the ducks in with the geese at night, but the latter were very territorial and kept throwing their weight around. By that time the ducks, being cleverer and smaller than the geese, had slipped through the fence and discovered the big pond out in the back pasture, and even the lure of grain in the evening was not enough to get them in to share quarters. The summer had passed and a steady parade of migrating mallards, wigeons, and buffleheads came to the pond; although they were unable to fly away with them, Bill and Joyce identified them as kin and soon didn't come into the barnyard at all. Winter came, and at night when the moon was full the howling of the coyotes came in through our bedroom window, sometimes as if they were just in the woodlot at the top of our farm. We lay awake, worried but helpless. We had failed at duck management by letting our pets go wild. It was small consolation that they were not alone out there: one day while trying to get them in, we disturbed a mallard hen that was nesting in the tussocks of grass and bushes near the edge of the pond.

In the middle of a March night I awoke suddenly and saw Christine silhouetted against the window. It had been clear overnight with a half moon riding high in the sky and a low silvery mist, lured from the earth by the cold night air, hanging just above the ground. "Joyce is quacking," she said. "There's something out there." When she threw the window open and yelled, a large dark shadow moved quickly away from the pond — then another one.

Joyce's loud quacking continued. I threw on some clothes and rushed blearily out into the night.

The moonlight was bright enough to see where I was going. The coyotes had vanished. With only a little searching, I came upon Bill lying in the grass, obviously nabbed before he could make it to safety in the pond; a few steps farther along I came upon the nesting mallard hen, half eaten, her eggs broken and smeared. Sitting duck, I thought. There was nothing else to do, so I went inside and went back to bed.

When dawn came, I walked the boundaries to check that there were no coyotes left lurking in the field, turned the animals out of their pens, and returned to the pond. To my surprise, Bill was alive and swimming very slowly near the end of the pond with Joyce quacking and zooming around him. After breakfast we decided to mount a rescue campaign: with a long pole and no pants on, I painfully eased myself into the chilly pond and gently herded Bill toward the shallows; as he tried to get away from me onto the bank he faltered and I was able to grab him and carry him, with Joyce waddling along behind, toward the Little Goose Coop. Christine had gathered some straw and water and we laid him down and examined him. Amazingly there were only a few dishevelled feathers and we could not find any puncture marks. His thick feathering had protected him, but he had no doubt been shaken violently, the way a rag is shaken by a terrier, and was on the point of going into shock.

Throughout the day we watched him. He sat very quietly, occasionally looking around, but he wasn't drinking any water — a bad omen for a duck. When we came out the following morning he was dead. Joyce quacked to be let out as usual but lingered at the gate, in the hope that Bill would follow, before returning to the pond. For the next two days, she stood on the bank and called for him. She was heartbroken. We buried Bill and planted a rosebush over him while we pondered our next move.

Several days later, when I was driving through the countryside, I spotted a sign nailed to a power pole advertising DUCKS and a phone number (the goose lady had only had Pekins, the white duck of the restaurant trade, and we had fallen for the handsome Khaki Campbells). At the next country store there was a phone booth; my call was answered by a woman who said she had a lot of young drakes for $10 each, and I could come by and get one. A few kilometres away, I arrived at a clone of the place where we had bought Hilary and Bev a couple of years before. It was a sea of mud, like the Somme in 1916, with a shallow pond in the middle and flocks of birds divided out by fence lines of loosely strung chicken wire. The smell of manure and crowding-induced stress was almost overpowering.

The owner was a chatty, friendly soul and asked me if I had any good recipes for duck. I recommended *canard à l'orange* — I think I actually said "duck with oranges" — as a restaurant dish but confessed I had found it rather greasy to cook. Anyway, I wanted the Khaki Campbell as a mate for my old, bereft duck. "We keep them because they eat slugs," I told her.

"Yeah," she said, looking out onto the mud, "we don't have any problem with slugs here, either." Or things growing, I thought. We went through a wire gate and waded into the flock of panic-stricken drakes; I came up with one and she another, but neither of them had the right look. So round they went in the compound as we herded them again toward the corner. In the ensuing scrum I came up with a beauty, a matinée-idol of a drake with a pale green bill and a long neck. Joyce will have no trouble bonding with this guy, I thought.

I was only slightly wrong. The new drake, whom Christine named Bruce, proved a bit immature for such a worldly duck as Joyce, and for the first while she merely tolerated him tagging along. She indulged in a brief fling with a wayward mallard we dubbed Marlon — because he was the wild one — but true to type he loved her and left her. By that time, Bruce had learned the moves and Joyce succumbed to his easy, quacking charm.

The question now was one of management. We booted Hilary

and Beverley out of Fort Goose and confined them at night in the barn, where they quickly became settled and happy. With much rattling of a grain bucket, Joyce and Bruce were enticed into a routine that brought them in at dusk and locked them into Fort Goose, where they settled and nested. All were happy under the new system. Freedom is a relative term when you're a farm animal. There's no point in being a free spirit and paying the price Bill paid. We'll leave that for the wild ones, who at least can fly from danger unless, like the dead mallard with all her broken eggs, fate marks them as dinner for someone stronger.

Fowl Business

<+ +>

Practically all broilers and most meat birds are reared in confinement,
so as to have absolute control of the feed intake, more rapid and
efficient growth, and better finish.

— Leonard Mercia, *Raising*
Poultry the Modern Way, 1975

THE BROODY HENS in our laying flock produced a supply of spring chickens, just like on a traditional farm. To renew the flock we kept the pullets, and to reduce the intensity of barnyard warfare we ate the cockerels after they had reached the age of five or six months. As eating chickens they were tasty if not especially tender; the white meat was a little skimpy compared with the big slab of standard restaurant fare, but the legs and wings were delicious. Either these cockerels were the wrong breed to produce a lot of breast meat, or else they underwent too much exercise to develop plump and tender flesh. One advantage was that, compared with fatty commercial chickens, they were easy to barbecue — there was no need to keep the fire extinguisher close at hand.

Fashions in chicken eating have changed a lot over the years. It is now rare to find a roasted chicken on a restaurant menu or at a friend's dinner party, as most people now express a preference for boneless chicken breast with some kind of sauce on it. Eating boneless breast meat doesn't require the concentration that dark meat does, allowing conversation to continue unimpeded. With the regrettable demise of the practice of wiping the hands on the pants, eating legs and wings has passed out of favour.

Chicken supply became an issue for us because our layabout laying hens were not producing enough spring chickens to fill the freezer for the winter. So one day while out on errands, I made a detour to the local hatchery and inquired about what kind of meat chicks they had for sale. The attendant gave me a photocopied brochure that featured what it described as a broiler chicken, a hybrid called the Cornish Giant. "Ready for Market in 7 Weeks," it claimed, and described the feed and conditions required to achieve this stupendous growth rate. I went from there to the co-op and asked about broiler feed.

"There are three kinds for the three stages," the young man in the warehouse told me. "Medicated Broiler Starter, Medicated Broiler Grower, and Broiler Finisher." The labels contained information on protein levels and the diseases that the medication would control. The Medicated Broiler Grower label contained the ominous warning: DO NOT FEED WITHIN SIX DAYS OF PROCESSING.

With all this information in hand, I went home to do some reading. My farm books from the 1920s and earlier made no mention of a creature called a broiler chicken. They talked about different breeds of chickens, described the lean and mean spring chicken that grew to about three pounds (one kilogram) at maturity, and gave directions on how to caponize (castrate) cockerels in order to produce plump roasting chickens of about four to five pounds (one and a half to two kilograms). However, *Raising Poultry the Modern Way*, first published in the 1970s, gave a slightly different description of chicken raising: it talked about "floor or litter management systems" and the health problems of birds reared in cages. Some further reading led me to publications of the U.S. Department of Agriculture, which had developed the broiler chicken in the late 1920s. This winged pig, which was bred to have a ravenous appetite and rapid growth rate, evolved after the White Leghorn had come to dominate egg production — because the male leghorn had little value for meat and had to be thrown away, a new chicken, the successor to the cockerels of the old dual-purpose farm breeds, had to be invented.

Although the broiler bird was a success, poultry farmers were forced initially to keep their operations fairly small, as were egg producers. Like the Irish potatoes of the 1840s, monocultures of chickens in a confined area were susceptible to plagues, generally of coccidiosis, Marek's disease, or Newcastle disease. Kimber Farms of Fremont, California, developed a series of vaccines during the 1930s and 1940s, but the real breakthrough occurred in the 1950s when Merck Pharmaceutical introduced the first effective coccidiostat.

Thanks to this development, both chicken and egg production and processing could be vertically integrated and industrialized. Pioneers of the industry included a Kansas produce hauler named John Tyson, who bought up grain farms and added a mill to feed his chickens, and developed a business with annual sales of more than $5 billion. Another was Frank Perdue, who developed the Oven Stuffer roaster chicken, which he patented in 1977 and advertised on radio and TV with the slogan, "It takes a tough man to make a tender chicken." Egg producers had found they could stimulate laying hens' pituitary glands, and thus their egg production, by raising their birds in windowless buildings with lights blazing for as much as 20 hours a day. Similarly, broiler raising became a year-round operation — with one season exactly the same as the next — in which the chickens were raised from hatching to market size in six to seven weeks using high-protein, medicated feeds. Usually science was able to keep a step ahead of nature, but occasionally nature fought back: for example, a particularly virulent form of Newcastle disease swept through the chickens of California in 1972, resulting in the extermination of more than nine million of them.

The old idea of caponizing cockerels had been tried chemically using DES (diethylstilbestrol), but the U.S. Food and Drug Administration banned it in 1959 after a restaurant worker who had eaten some chicken necks containing DES residue was observed to have developed "feminizing traits." A further evolution of the broiler came in 1980 when McDonald's introduced Chicken McNuggets and created a huge demand: Tyson Foods developed a larger bird, dubbed Mr. McDonald's, to cut down on deboning costs. In only a couple of generations, chicken (and, to a lesser extent, turkey) had become a low-cost diet staple of North Americans. Perhaps only the potato has such a wide (and widening) effect on the consumer market.

For us the idea of raising chickens on broiler feed, let alone eating the result, held little appeal. All our country acquaintances had stories about broiler chickens. Deprived of exercise, they grow so quickly on the mix of high-protein feed, with its growth enhancers like those used by Eastern European weight lifters, that they can hardly stand because their bone development can't keep pace with their weight gain. A typical problem is the self-explanatory blackleg, which is prompted by these factors. Commonly, broiler chickens are susceptible to bursting a major heart artery, causing another condition cleverly labelled "flip-over" in which they leap in the air and land on their backs dead. They have to be debeaked to reduce cannibalism, and any sudden fright can cause piling (also a problem with turkeys) and the crushing and smothering (followed by the eating) of the unlucky ones on the bottom, and so on. As you can guess, we were soon a lot of fun at dinner parties. A conversation that began innocently with someone asking, "And what's new on the farm?" would trail off into silence broken only by the sound of forks and knives being put down around the table.

The question was: could broiler chickens be raised more naturally? Determined to find out, I ordered 50 day-old Cornish Giants — little peeping yellow fluffy chicks, different from the purebreds we had raised because of their colour and, also, their very large feet, some of which featured oddly twisted toes. They weren't debeaked and I wasn't about to do it. Just like the other chicks had, they scratched about on the floor of the old rabbit hutch under-

neath the infrared lamps, filled their beaks with water and swallowed
it by tipping their heads back and, within a few days, began to grow
feathers at their wing tips. Compared with the others, though, they
were wildly enthusiastic about the groceries and ate till they had
emptied the little feeders, then slouched around moodily till I
showed up with more; the others had scratched and explored, and
usually spread the grits around on the floor to peck at later.

After much consideration, it seemed to me that the central issue
was to slow down their growth rate from the breakneck pace created
by the broiler feeds. I decided to feed them Chick Starter, a slightly
less rich and additive-free brew than Broiler Starter, which was
intended for raising commercial laying hens like the Isa Browns we
had had years before. Nevertheless, they wolfed it down and a few of
them flipped. I switched them to Chick Grower, a lower-protein
mix intended for birds weeks older than they, and it seemed to settle them down a bit. The weather was warm and soon I opened the
door and let them roam outside, protected from the curious hens
and Arthur by a wire fence. Before long they were behaving like real
chickens, scratching around and sleeping in the shade of the cot-
tonwood tree in the middle of the run. However, gravity was a major
concern for them and I did not bother trying to show them how to
perch – they were too big and clumsy.

Six weeks had gone by and they were nowhere near maturity,
probably weighing little more than about half a kilogram each. This
was good. A casual conversation with Jan about sheep feeds led me
to a nearby farm that grew barley, oats, and wheat; the farmer, Ken,
with his balding pate and shoulder-length hair, looked like a
refugee from a communal jug band but, in fact, had a university
degree in agriculture and was the fifth generation of his family to
farm that land. He had some barley left from his last year's crop that
he was willing to run through his oat roller to break it down and
make it more digestible for the winged pigs. I supplemented that
with piles of weeds from the garden and discovered that they loved

stinging nettles. They grew slowly as they marched around in the sunshine, sometimes flapping their wings as they walked. Their legs became very long compared with those of the commercial chickens I had eaten over the years, presumably because they were getting their exercise.

One day a boyhood pal from the city dropped by, bringing with him a few bottles of beer he had brewed at a mutual friend's beer-making plant. He was carrying with him a plastic bag full of what looked like wet grain.

"You know Howie does a lot of all-grain brewing," Brian said. "It all gets thrown out once it's been boiled to make the wort. It seems like such a waste. We were talking about your animals and wondering whether they'd eat it."

"Well, I've got these chickens...."

We walked across the barnyard, the plastic bag attracting the attention of the patrolling hens and geese, and got to the fence around the winged pigs' run. As one they surged forward, reminding us of the old saying: "Does the name Pavlov ring a bell?" When I scooped out half the grain with my hand and threw it in, it caused a ruckus like a fumble on the one-yard line. The other half of the bag drew the same response. The following day I was on the phone to Howie, who was delighted to reduce the amount of garbage he had to pay to dump. I took him some hastily purchased garbage cans and soon had a steady supply of about 100 kilograms of wet grain a week!

Jan was interested to hear that I was feeding brewery grain. "It's good sheep feed, too," he told me. "Like silage — it's a little bit fermented, which is good for their rumens." He described to me how, as a boy in Holland, he used to see the Heineken truck going from place to place selling brewery grain to the dairy farmers. "It's a good supplement," he said. "It's mainly the starch that's missing, and the price is certainly right." I decided to make a permanent arrangement for the stuff, even after the meat chickens were finito, and use it through the winter for the sheep and the laying chickens.

By the time they were about three months old most of the Cornish Giants had matured into quite handsome birds, except for their big clown feet, which caused them to walk without the easy grace of a normal chicken. They looked almost demure with their bright red combs and wattles and their snowy-white feathers. However, their behaviour at feeding time, which was almost always, resembled that of the eager Visigoths at the gates of Rome. They crowded around me when I entered the run and, in their excitement, pecked and bit my feet and calves. As I bent over toward a feeder (a piece of old eaves trough nailed to the side of the hutch) with a bucket of grain in an outstretched arm, a dozen or more of them would fly at it with a wild, wailing cry, almost knocking the bucket from my hand and leaving my arm bruised and blood-blistered from misplaced chomping. Without doubt, it was time for them to go.

But how to slaughter them? Plucking and cleaning chickens out-doors is not *that* unpleasant if you have a comfortable stool in the shade with a breeze to keep the flies away, but at a maximum you can do about three an hour. Do 50, and dig a huge hole in the garden to bury the feathers and guts, and you've more or less ruined your week. There were a couple of processing plants around, but I was warned by a country acquaintance that they were geared to the big producers and sometimes you got somebody else's chickens instead of your own. No way to that, I thought. I had almost run out of options when it was suggested I call a local guy named Al who made house calls.

The voice on the other end of the line was youthful and well spo-ken. "Sure," he said, "we can come by. Just let me look at my calen-dar here…. How about next Wednesday morning first thing? Okay? Don't feed them at dawn … we just need power and water, and you have to have enough buckets and containers to cool them all down in. Right. See you then!" Executions are always at dawn, I thought as I hung up the phone.

On the appointed morning, which was cool but promised a hot sun, I kept the white chickens locked up and Arthur and his gang

confined to their run. At about five after seven, an odd-looking
pickup truck made the turn onto our road and was at the gate a
minute later. A tall, blond young man got out. His hair was neatly
trimmed, styled a little long at the back; he looked fit and healthy like
a young athlete, maybe a hockey player. I walked over and we shook
hands. "Hi, I'm Al!" he said brightly. He didn't introduce his assistant, a more scrofulous character who nevertheless had a friendly
smile. "Where are they?" Al asked. I pointed toward the rabbit hutch.
He climbed back into the truck and backed over to the fence.

Quickly and efficiently the two men set up their mobile plant.
The pickup truck was a large GMC model with the normal pickup bed
replaced by a custom-made flat deck, all stainless steel and shiny in
the morning sun. On it were a small chopping block at the back, a
row of steel cones above a draining trough on one side, a water-
filled vat heated by natural gas (which also powered the truck) on the
other, a short stainless-steel table beside it, and a large hooded contraption, containing a drum studded with black rubber things that
looked like suction cups, against the truck's cab. They swung out
four outriggers to stabilize the deck and placed a large plastic barrel
on each of them. Al fired up the gas flame under the vat, which had
been preheated and was already steaming, and checked the temperature on a thermometer built into the side, while his assistant
plugged in the hooded contraption, checked the revolving drum,
and filled the barrels with water. They put on ankle-length oilskin
aprons and rubber gloves, hosed themselves off, and cleaned their
knives. "You can start bringing the birds now," said Al.

Never have I experienced such carnage. Even my memories of
Sam Peckinpah movies paled into insignificance. My role was to
push my way into the old hutch and emerge with a couple of ter-
rorized, squawking chickens hanging by a leg in each hand, swing
the door shut with a foot, and hand them up to Al. He expertly
lopped off their heads and stuffed each body, still quivering and
jerking violently, neck down in a cone to drain. A brief pause while

he killed others, and then he pulled the drained birds out of the cones and, taking a single step across the truck, dropped them into the vat of hot water to loosen their feathers. While I handed him more victims, his assistant pulled the birds from the vat and, holding them by their feet, rotated them against the revolving drum of the hooded contraption, which plucked the feathers neatly. Finally he tossed the plucked birds into the water barrel to cool and went back for more. They said little to each other except for an occasional, almost monosyllabic comment about some movie they had both seen.

The killing settled down to a steady pace. Occasionally I would hear through the fog of pitiful squawking and dust and flying feathers the muffled comment, "Need more birds," or "Need water on them birds." But within about 20 minutes they were all dead, plucked, and cooling. A weird calm descended over the hutch and run that had been so frenetic the previous day; birds sang in the hedgerow and the sheep moved about on the pasture in the distance. Al and his assistant hosed off their aprons and the back of the truck.

"Fill your buckets now," Al commanded me, while he and the assistant began to pull chickens out of the barrels and swiftly clean them. He seemed now to be more relaxed, with the difficult job done, and told me in response to my questions that he was 27 and had been killing chickens for money since he was 14: "My dad had to drive me to jobs for the first few years," he laughed. Isn't 14 young to settle on a career path, I suggested? "Oh, I'd been doing it since I was nine. My father used to kill chickens for local people when he wasn't too busy farming. One day I went along with him and found I was good at it."

By eight o'clock they were done and hosing everything off. My 50 chickens, all cleaned and plucked, lay underwater in the buckets, cooling down slowly so they would freeze properly. The assistant pulled a pail from beneath the end of the drain trough and started toward some blackberry bushes. He stopped and turned around.

93

"You want this blood on your bushes?" he asked with a smile. "Why not," I replied coolly. The bill came to $1.10 a bird, with a $10 travelling charge. "See you next year," Al smiled as they drove through the gate and on to their next job. "If you ever have just a few to do, we're at home every Thursday — you can just bring 'em by."

Next year? I thought as I spent the day packing the birds into extra-large freezer bags, then weighing them and pricing them. We had told a handful of friends what we were doing and, between them, they had snapped up the 25 we wanted to sell at free-range prices. The balance went into our freezer. Next year? I wondered as I cleaned the foul manure and mess from the old hutch, a gas mask on my face to protect me from the ammonia.

But the memory of that morning had faded by the time we started to eat the chickens. They were the best I had ever tasted, whether grilled on a barbecue (where they didn't catch fire), baked or simmered or whatever. Our friends called back and asked if we had any more. We got some calls from strangers asking if they could buy chicken from us. By the following spring I had planned a better system of feeding them and hooked up automatic waterers to reduce the amount of daily labour. Howie's brewing business had picked up and he had lots of grain he wanted to get rid of. And then, one day in early April, I went to the hatchery and picked up a hundred day-old Cornish Giant chicks. We were back in the chicken business again.

Making Hay
‹+ +›

When the sunne shineth, make hay.
— John Heywood, *Proverbes*, 1546

IN SUMMER AND FALL, the sounds and smells of hay making dominate our valley. During the spring, the grass grows tall in the hay fields and eventually its pretty panicles develop and open. The grasses nod in the breeze. Often the sky is a bright, transparent blue, dotted with cumulus clouds. Shadows move rapidly across the fields, sometimes from a passing cloud, other times because a wave of wind moves like a shadow through the grass. The fields are cut, the grass cures in the sunshine, and with tedding and turning it becomes hay ready for baling. Its smell carries on the wind. Elsewhere cows and calves, sheep and lambs roam about, surfeited with rich grass but seeking favourite spots for a special treat like a diner examining the dessert tray in a restaurant. Ruminants love to roam and are experts at grass identification.

The best hay comes from pastures modified from their natural state — although civilization began in tandem with the development of a stable food supply, mainly due to the cultivation of grains, many centuries passed before the Romans began improving pastures. An understanding of clovers, which are an important element of a balanced pasture, only became common in the 17th century. Not surprisingly, the arts of pasture management and hay making, essential to keeping stock alive through the winter, developed mainly in the regions where livestock couldn't graze through the winter. Agricultural literature, such as John Fitzherbert's *Boke of Husbandrye* (1523), Thomas Tusser's *Hundreth Good Pointes of Husbandrie* (1557), the above-mentioned "proverbes" of John Heywood (1546), and the Germanic farm lore Barnaby Googe collected as *Foure Bookes of Husbandrie* (1586), gave a lot of advice on haying and pasturing.

It was cheaper for us to buy hay than to make our own — we had too little land, our fields were too small and oddly shaped for modern equipment, and we didn't own the proper mower, tedder, and baler combination (let alone the tractor) to do the job. I did have the Medieval Man Machine, an Austrian scythe with a hammered-steel blade, and became relatively adept at cutting tall grass with it, but it would have taken all my time — truly from dawn to dusk through the season — to scythe a few acres, ted and turn the hay by hand in the hot sun, rake it into windrows, then put it up into cocks for further curing before hauling it into the barn. That, after all, was the medieval experience: unless you were a noble, you worked yourself half to death in order to avoid dying of starvation. It's hard not to romanticize those days, eh?

Our neighbour across the road, Bill, did a high-tech version of my scything. He had a number of horses, including a pair of huge Belgian draft horses, that he had trained into harness for pulling wagons and carts for everything from hayrides to wedding coaches. Along the way he had picked up some horse-drawn implements, including a mower and a tedder, and every spring he cut one of his fields with horsepower. It was so picturesque and blessedly quiet compared with the thumping din of a tractor, the only sound being his commands to the horses and the clicking of the sickle-bar through the grass. When the hay cured, he hitched two horses to his big wagon and, with a pitchfork, loaded the loose hay. Although it was only a fraction of the hay he needed for the year, it provided exercise and unbeatable pleasure, the latter even for his neighbours.

Jan was the best source of information on hay, as on most things. "Look at the field when the grasses are in flower," he said. "Look for the variety. You want a field with the right combination of grasses that'll all be ripe at the same time. There shouldn't be a seed head in the field when the hay is cut." He recommended that I make the acquaintance of a farmer named Mel just up the road, so I went there one afternoon late in May, introduced myself, and said I was looking to buy some hay. We looked out past a field of grazing cattle, a field planted to oats and another planted to corn, to his hay field stretching away as far as a screen of trees in the distance. In the warm sun, the air seemed to buzz with the fullness of spring.

"We'll cut in a week," he said, "depending on the weather forecast. You got sheep? You'll want to wait for second cut." I asked what the difference was. "It's softer on their mouths. Cows and horses don't care, but sheep are happiest with second. Or third, if it's a good year. Less waste, but anything they won't eat of first cut makes good bedding." I don't want to buy bedding at hay prices, I thought, and told him I'd wait for second.

I went home to read about hay in my old farm books. One quoted Pliny: "Meadow land will grow old in time and it requires to be renovated every now and then, by sowing upon it a crop of beans, or else rape or millet, after which it should be sown the next year with corn, and then left for hay the third." Another was published by the Dominion of Canada in 1913 to educate prospective farmers: entitled *Fodder and Pasture Plants*, it was something of a cure for insomnia, if the truth be told, but it contained a lot of information on native grasses and the common, introduced ones from

Europe, such as timothy and perennial ryegrass. Clover is necessary as a replenisher of nitrogen into the soil, it stated, as many grasses are heavy feeders. The hay should be cut just at the point when the flower is fertilized, for at that time all of the nourishment collected by the plant is still in its stems and leaves; as soon as the seeds start to develop, they draw nourishment from the rest of the plant, which causes the stems to harden and become unpalatable. Rain was the enemy, as Heywood's epigram implied: when the grass was cut it contained about 80 percent moisture, but it had to be cured to about 15 percent or else it would moulder or, in the worst case, spontaneously ignite, causing "mow-burning" and a barn fire; a rain shower slowed the curing process, and the dampness robbed the hay of protein.

The Dominion book recommended short crop rotations for well-drained upland farms. "As soon as the hay crop of the second year is removed, the meadow may be ploughed and fallowed for the balance of the year to suppress weeds. An application of farmyard manure, shallow ploughed or worked into the surface soil, should fit the land for spring planting with a hoed or other cleaning crop, which may be followed by a nurse crop of cereal grains, and again seeded to Red Clover and grasses for two years of meadow and pasture." That was the 20th-century variation on "Turnip" Townshend's Norfolk four-course rotation.

But Mel's field looked too wet to be described as upland pasture, and he didn't appear to rotate his hay field with other crops. The book suggested that in wet, clayey soils it was expedient to leave the land as meadow for long periods, perhaps fertilizing it in the early spring with a dressing of well-rotted farm manure. However, it cautioned that "permanent pastures yield a small revenue when compared with thorough cultivation and alternate cropping."

I was curious about this statement and asked Jan whether many farmers plowed up their pasture and reseeded it, or whether Mel's permanent pasture was typical. He thought for a minute and then, translating from his boyhood Dutch school lessons, recalled the phrase: "Making the pasture black is farmer's work, but making it green is for the gentry."

"What does that mean?" I asked, baffled.

"It means you need money to make a good hay meadow — seed is really expensive, let alone drainage and fuel and the time to cultivate it properly."

He was interested in the advice from the Dominion of Canada book on short rotations and remembered that the Dutch farmers of his childhood, including his father, rotated crops on a seven-year cycle — he was sure because of the biblical significance of the number seven. They maximized their hay production by grazing the fields early in the spring: the grass, which really only wants to go to seed, was forced to spread and developed more leaf by being eaten down and delayed in its rush to maturity. A lot of current hay farmers, like many of those in our valley, had no livestock to keep the grass from going quickly to seed, and thus got a comparatively poor hay crop. But more important for them than yield was the modern reality that made time paramount — and equipment easier than livestock to leave over winter holidays — and skewed the economics of farming away from its traditions.

One piece of common sense from the Dominion book meshed with my lengthy childhood experience at mowing suburban lawns: when the grass was cut for hay it began to rejuvenate itself, just like the garden flowers that only continue to bloom if they're regularly deadheaded. I had believed that all I needed was the sheep — they would crop the grass and fertilize the pasture and all would be trouble-free. Jan set me straight: "The grass gets ahead of them — as soon as the stems get woody, they won't touch it, and it won't come back strongly enough to fatten them in the fall. As far as the grass is concerned, its job is done once it's set seed."

"But they've got lots of room to roam," I replied.

"That's a good thing, but eventually they won't find any young grass to eat. You'd be better off leaving it to grow and then brush

cutting it twice a year rather than having a lousy, trampled field."

"So they won't do well if I just leave the grass alone?" I asked unhappily, hoping against hope.

"Well, you've got to manage the land you've got. You could buy a lot more sheep and they'd keep the grass chewed down and fresh, but then you'd have to buy a lot more hay to feed them for the winter, and you still don't have enough land to justify buying haying equipment."

"So I should cut the fields."

"Mmm-hmmm."

With great reluctance, I began to search for a tractor. My only previous experience had been with Steve, Ed and Eleanor's old two-wheel-drive Massey-Ferguson tractor, which had seemed too big for some parts of our place yet too small for any serious cultivation. Did I need a four-wheel drive? How powerful should it be? What would its tasks be, beyond cutting the fields? Until that time I had managed to avoid buying motorized equipment, other than a small, tiller-steered rider mower with the confidence-inspiring brand name of Snapper — I used it to zoom around the vegetable garden and Christine's half-acre rose garden, but it was useless in tall grass or on rough terrain. In a country-life magazine, *Harrowsmith*, I had read a comparison test of small tractors that warned that they were like chain saws — you were dead before you realized you had made a mistake — but it also stated that the average North American farm tractor was 20 years old, implying that they were solidly built and that one did not have to purchase new. This was good, as the high-quality new ones were expensive, the smallest and simplest being about $15,000.

The more I found out about tractors the more I warmed to the idea of having one. But what did I need it for? My aching back suggested a few things: removing the plywoodlike mixture of manure and straw from the sheep pen was, not surprisingly, like one of the labours of Hercules; turning the big compost piles and moving

compost itself the hundred or so metres to parts of the garden was
another. Pushing the snow out of the driveway and barnyard in the
winter was a drag, too. All of these chores pointed to a small,
manoeuvrable machine with a front-end loader. A mower required
a three-point hitch on the back and a PTO — a power takeoff — as did
tilling, the great springtime backbreaker in the vegetable garden. I
could get mowers and rototillers for a small tractor, but any hay
baler or manure spreader required a fairly large tractor for power.

Back to the farm books I went, and learned that the modern tractor was developed largely by Harry Ferguson, an Irish aircraft designer
whose name has been on the sides of Massey-Ferguson machines for
all my life. Prior to his time, tractors had been enormous things, usually steam-powered with lugged steel wheels, that pulled plows or
reapers or threshers through the fields; they had a power drive on the
side that turned a long belt connected to a similar drive on the
thresher. The first commercially successful steam-powered thresher
had been introduced by Jerome Increase Case in 1843; almost 20
years later, steam-powered tractors began to replace horses on big
wheat farms. Gasoline tractors emerged at about the same time as the
Model T, which was, in its own way, the first practical farm vehicle for
the small operator (farmers jacked the back end off the ground and
ran mills and saws with a belt looped around a rear wheel). At the outbreak of the First World War, Ferguson was conscripted by the British
Ministry of Agriculture to maximize food supply. He observed that a
huge amount of grain that might otherwise be human food was used
for "power animals" instead, and he focused his attention on tractor
design. After years of work, he perfected the hydraulic control mech-
anism that allowed implements to be hung from the back of a tractor
and that raised and lowered them with ease; the front-end loader —
the bucket on the front of a tractor that can pick up and dump piles of
stuff — is also run by hydraulic power.

I phoned Ed and asked him if he would keep an eye out for a
suitable small tractor. He was willing to lend me Steve, but we agreed

that he had to do the same work at the same time and eventually
sharing wouldn't work. I scanned the papers and went to a couple of
auctions — foreclosures of farmers who had gotten into trouble buying tractors and implements — but found everything too big for my
needs. Then one afternoon Ed called to say that a member of the
road crew he had been working with had moved from an acreage to
a suburban lot; he had a small tractor with a rototiller and mower
sitting in his driveway, and his wife was after him to get rid of it. It
was an older model, 15-horsepower four-wheel-drive YANMAR, he
said, a diesel, and it sounded like it would be good. He was asking
six (thousand, that is), but Ed suggested I start at five. "A diesel's
good," he said, "they're more reliable and cheaper to run than gas."

The beat-up little tractor and its implements stood out from
the shiny cars on the suburban cul-de-sac. The owner was eager.
"I've got a case of oil you can have. Oh, and a pail of hydraulic fluid
here.... There's diesel in this can — here's the owner's manual." We
walked out into his driveway. The tractor was little, I thought, but it
looked sturdy. He got on it and turned the key. The diesel rattled
into life. I drove it back and forth in the driveway, moved the bucket
up and down, tried the hitch, and engaged the PTO. It all seemed to
work. "Third gear's gone in low range," cautioned the owner.
"Other than that she's fine." I hemmed and hawed, leading up to
my lowball offer with all the subtlety of a cavalry charge. "All I've got
is five thousand," I said. "It's a deal!" he exclaimed so quickly it took
me aback. He really did want to get rid of it. Uh-oh, I thought, too
late. But as it turned out, I needn't have worried.

Everything about the tractor and its implements seemed so new.
It needed greasing in all sorts of strange places, and tightening and
adjusting, but I had not sold the tools I had used 20 years earlier to
keep my old Volkswagen running. Although the little bit of
confidence I had remaining from those boy-mechanic days was
rather like fool's courage, to my amazement the tractor was such a
simple thing that I could understand without difficulty what it took

103

to maintain it. It was a far cry even from the cars of the 1970s, which had become so complex I had hung up my tools in despair.

The implements were heavy and, with their revolving blades, scary. The mower weighed about 200 kilograms and was covered with warning stickers, mainly pictograms showing hands being chopped off and bodies wrapped around revolving shafts. It was so heavy that it had to be levered onto the three-point hitch using two-by-fours as pry-bars. It was called a brush cutter, not the sort of sickle-bar mower I had seen farmers use for their hay, and had a flat steel deck more than a metre long concealing a single large blade, which was clutch-mounted and hinged so that it would swing out of the way if it hit something hard. With the tractor running flat-out in a low gear, it was able to cut waist-high grass. I mowed the fields slowly over a few days, a couple of hours in the morning, a long break to let the sinuses settle down, then a couple more hours in the afternoon. All the rough grass that the sheep had ignored and trampled was cleaned off, and the place soon looked like a park. Joe even stopped his manure spreader and walked over to the fence to call out: "Fields look great!" It's sort of like suburbanites and their lawns, I thought — a tidy farmer is a good neighbour. I found that the sheep were grateful and resumed eating in a more systematic way, and that if I left the grass to grow into the fall it remained in tussocks that gave them some fairly good winter fodder.

Early in September, Mel called to say he was doing a second cut, and if I pulled the bales out of the field I could have them for 50 cents cheaper than if I bought them out of his barn. Three loads on the pickup truck later and I had 75 bales in the barn, which sounds effortless, but it was several days later when my back stopped aching. The bales were about 20 kilograms each and, although I had seen people casually pitch them high into the air, it was a technique difficult to master. G. F. Warren, writing *Farm Management* in 1913, knew as much: "Many persons, who are not closely in touch with farming, believe that the introduction of machinery has done away with the necessity for strength and skill in manual operations, but these will always be very important considerations for the farmer." He noted that "it takes thousands of efforts for the boy to learn to throw a baseball straight, [and] apparently it is just as difficult to learn to pitch hay." (At this point, it is worth repeating one of the few known jokes about hay: A visiting farmer says to another farmer, "In my county they're going to ban them round bales." "How come?" "Cows can't get a square meal!")

In the barn, with the bales stacked high, the smell was of autumn and the harvest. It only remained to get grain for the chickens and some straw for bedding before winter set in.

Ken called and said he had combine-harvested his wheat and barley; it was in his granary and he would be sacking it soon, but in the meantime did I want straw for bedding? I went over on a cloud-less afternoon late in September and drove around his huge field, while skeins of geese passed by overhead on the way south. The straw bales lay where his machine had dropped them. They were golden-coloured compared with the green-buff hay, and they were light and easy to pitch compared with the hay bales.

Back at the farm, in the raking golden sunlight of autumn after-noons, we spent every possible moment sitting by the pond. The barn swallows, which through the summer had been constantly in the sky, acrobatically picking off insects and skimming low over the water, sometimes skipping off the surface like flat stones to cool their breasts, gradually slipped away, until there were only one or two left.

"I am waited for in Egypt...," Christine quoted the swallow bid-ding farewell to Oscar Wilde's Happy Prince. Soon they were gone. Migrating mallards, along with a few pintails and wigeons, overnighted on the pond. The long grass around the edge had faded to a pale buff colour, and the leaves of the maples and cottonwoods had changed to their autumn hues.

The older sheep, who forget nothing, began to hang around near the barn in the evening and fixed me with the sort of knowing look only old sheep are capable of. They had spent the summer in the pasture, sleeping under the stars and starting to graze at dawn, no doubt imagining themselves to be the brave sheep of yore, but now hay was on their minds. Eric had spent the summer in a separate field and we had considered getting a wether (which Christine proposed to name Stormy) to keep him company but had in the end picked up an old ewe from a friend instead. We kept them apart from the rest of the ewes until late in October, ensuring that the next year's lambs would be born no earlier than late March when the grass would once again be green and rich.

We drained the water lines and put the garden to bed. Some of the chickens began to moult, the traditional sign that it was time to plant winter crops like fall rye and durum wheat. Pumpkins ripened and the autumn rains began. With hay in the barn, we were ready for winter.

Putting Food By

<+ +>

A succession of fresh vegetables from early spring is necessary for the health of all classes in this country.

— William Rennie, Sr., *Rennie's*
Agriculture in Canada, 1916

It was one thing to make sure we had enough winter fodder for the animals, and another to ensure that there was enough for us. To go along with the chicken and lamb in the freezer, and eggs from the hens, there had to be vegetables stored and ready to eat. Although it was easy to grow vegetables for summer meals, in our ideal farm there would be food put by for the winter: potatoes, onions, shallots, garlic, and cabbage would be hardened off and root-cellared; summer crops like basil, broccoli, cauliflower, and beans would be processed and frozen; apples would be dried and berries turned into jams; hardy root crops like leeks, carrots, and parsnips would stay in the ground, ready to be dug out even from under the snow; and hardy leaf vegetables like spinach and rapini would tough it through the winter with some straw bedding around them for protection and emerge to give us fresh greens as soon as spring sunshine warmed the ground. As it turned out, there were always wild greens, most notably stinging nettles, that were up before the domestic ones and made memorable quiches — in farm talk, pies — adapted from pioneer recipe books.

In the midst of the plenty of modern agriculture, with vegetables delivered fresh from both distant lands and heated greenhouses to markets open 24 hours a day, it perhaps seems foolish and atavistic to attempt to feed oneself year-round with the produce from a northern summer. Perspective on the matter was provided by Janet Greene who, in the introduction to the food preservers' Bible, *Putting Food By,* defined the verb "to put by" as "an old, deep-country way of saying to 'save something you don't have to use now, against the time when you'll need it.' Putting food by is the antidote for running scared." To us growing food and attempting to feed ourselves through the winter was a stab at self-reliance in an increasingly interdependent world – a way of saying to ourselves, in the face of pending social and economic collapse, that somehow we would have the skills to carry on.

To everything there is a season. The sheep know that, and modify their behaviour around the great cycles of nature; they make it through the winter and arrive at springtime thin, with a hankering for fresh green grass; their instinct and the fecundity of summer fattens them before winter, oblivious to the market's demand for lean meat. They sleep more in the winter, as do the chickens. But for most people today, there is little real change in their lives from season to season. There are few foods that they can't get and don't eat year-round: tomatoes are fresh, if tasteless, in every season; fresh chicken is always available, but it is not the tasty "spring chicken" of an earlier era. Seasonal cooking, with the exception perhaps of berry pies and corn on the cob, is now a rarity in much of North America.

As for whether growing your own food is worth it, whatever that means, we turned again to the authors of *Putting Food By*. Analysing the question from a straight dollars-and-cents standpoint, their answer was an emphatic no. But they went on to consider the matter of personal satisfaction. "Through the garden and later preserving," they wrote, "one teaches one's children that planting (birth), growing and harvesting (maturing) and cutting-back and plowing-under (dying) are the continuity of all living things, and nothing ever is a waste." The agronomist Sir Albert Howard, who spent 30 years of his career in India, came to the same conclusion, and wrote in *An Agricultural Testament* that "Mother Nature never tries to farm without livestock; she always raises mixed crops; great pains are taken to preserve the soil and to prevent erosion; the mixed animal and vegetable wastes are converted into humus; there is no waste; the processes of growth and of decay balance one another...." Our friend Jan had yet another angle on growing your own food: he buried his dead sheep in the vegetable garden and every summer, with his urban grandchildren helping, he prepared a small bed and planted a patch of wheat; together they watered it and tended it, then harvested it, threshed it, and ground it into flour. They saved the best to plant the following year. "I tell them: 'That's where your daily bread comes from, and don't you forget it,'" he said.

The techniques of preserving food took a long time to develop. Until the 18th century, most people were farmers and most of those just scraped by, their granaries barely managing to keep them alive until spring. In the early 18th century in England, the innovations of "Turnip" Townshend, who followed the Dutch and Flemish practice of keeping animals alive through the winter on a diet of turnips, made fresh meat available at all times of the year. A parallel development introduced methods to cheat the climate, especially in the great country houses of England where gardeners managed to keep vegetables in production throughout the year. Some of these techniques had been around for generations, including the

Clos Normand (the kitchen garden with high brick walls that stored daytime heat and protected the crops from wind), the classic hotbed that used fresh manure to force tender crops such as lettuce, and the cold frame for starting seeds early in the spring. In the television series *The Victorian Kitchen Garden,* Harry Dodson, who apprenticed on a country estate in the 1920s, demonstrated how sophisticated an operation vegetable and fruit production at the great English country houses had become. All of that fell into disuse when modern transportation technology and cold storage became common after the Second World War.

Although the rich had ice at their disposal in summer for aeons, the middle class only got it early in the 19th century when New England businessmen began to harvest ice from frozen ponds and store it in sawdust icehouses. Concurrently iceboxes became commercially available, the first patent going in 1803 to a Maryland farmer named Thomas Moore. In 1846 Henry David Thoreau noted in his journal that Walden Pond had yielded 10,000 pounds (4,500 kilograms) of ice in 16 days. In those years, tons of New England ice was shipped all over the world, with enough of it arriving, even after voyages of several months, to places like India to turn a profit. Mechanical refrigeration was developed soon thereafter: Ferdinand Carré took his invention, which used liquid ammonia in its compressor, to the 1862 London exhibition and made blocks of ice that dazzled the crowds. Technological progress was so rapid that two decades later a shipment of frozen beef and mutton made it successfully from Australia to England. But the limiting factor in the spread of mechanical refrigeration was the slow spread of electrification; only about 10 percent of American homes were wired for electricity at the turn of the 20th century, so horse-drawn ice-delivery wagons were still a common sight in towns and cities.

During the 1920s and 1930s, consumer demand for refrigeration increased, and a combination of technological improvements and mass production reduced the price of a refrigerator from about

$600 in 1920 to less than $175 in 1939. The freezer gained wider acceptance following the discoveries of Clarence Birdseye who, during an extended stay in Labrador, Newfoundland, worked on freezing cabbages in barrels of seawater. In 1925 he developed the deep-freezing process for cooked foods that formed the basis of the modern convenience-food industry.

The lakeside cottage community where I spent my childhood summers had a common icehouse — even as late as the 1950s and 1960s getting away from it all meant getting away from electricity, too. One of my least pleasant summer tasks was carrying the ice bucket and a shovel to the icehouse, a crudely constructed shed of old boards, and digging through the scratchy sawdust to find a block of ice that had been packed there during the depths of winter. However, electricity soon arrived along the lake and the core group of cottagers, who lived permanently in a nearby town and who organized the ice-harvesting party in the winter, decided to wire their houses. My parents didn't, buying ice from the town for a year or so before installing a propane fridge.

For many people, preserving food means processing it and putting it in jars or cans, a procedure that dates back to the early part of the 19th century and the invention of tin-plated cans and the technique of soldering. At first canning had its broadest application in the fishing industry, with canned salmon from British Columbia, Washington, and Alaska being shipped all over the world. The Mason jar, now a generic term like Xerox or Kleenex, was patented by a man named (not surprisingly) John L. Mason, and it reduced the amount of spoilage for farm families who had previously relied on pickle barrels, sauerkrauts, and root cellars for their winter food supply.

First, though, the food had to be grown, and it was soon evident that a country vegetable garden had three advantages over the city ones we had kept: light, space, and availability of fertilizer. Our city gardens had always been enclosed by the shadows of tall houses and greenery, reducing the amount of light available, and pollution

made the air less transparent to sunlight (our local government estimated crop losses in areas downwind from the city at 20 percent).
The city garden was always cramped: it was easy to plant the rows of
vegetables just a little too close together, robbing them of root
space, water, and sunshine; space was always at such a premium that
it became difficult even to turn a wheelbarrow or make compost,
and it was hard to justify the allocation for winter-keeper crops like
potatoes (which were comparatively cheap to buy) when we could
grow expensive delicacies such as basil.

In the country, we mixed sheep and chicken manure with the
garden weeds and waste and were soon producing a potent compost.
Henry Jackson Waters's *The New Agriculture,* published in 1924, recommended the application of from 500 to 600 pounds (225 to
270 kilograms) of manure per year on a 10- by 15-metre garden;
ours was soon twice that big, but we had lots of manure. The source
of bonemeal was the dead creatures that from time to time had to be
disposed of, usually newborn lambs that didn't make it and chickens that fell over dead for some inscrutable reason. On this diet, the
soil improved to a fine tilth and the garden flourished. Every year I
dug it larger but still found that we ran out of garlic or could have
used more corn for fattening market lambs and chickens.

The big problem was root-cellaring. The authors of *Putting Food
By* described root-cellaring as the only food-preservation method
that had not been improved upon during the 20th century, and
they blamed this on the changing nature of house construction —
the warm, dry basement has replaced the cool, damp cellar of the
old farmhouse. Our house had a cool, dry crawl space that worked
not badly, so that by the end of the winter we still had some edible
potatoes. One year I packed carrots in sand and they lasted until late
February and then turned to the consistency of spoiled cream. The
next year I left them in the ground, which doesn't freeze hard in our
valley, and they were doing well until a vole came along and ate them
all from below, leaving only the orange cap and the fronds.

The final element of our ideal traditional garden was the type of seeds. The modern hybrid ones available at every garden store gave good vegetables, but the seed from the best of them did not grow into anything at all the following year. Only the old-fashioned heritage seeds, available from specialty growers, had the ability to regenerate themselves year after year, even though the yields of some varieties were not as massive as were those of the hybrids. We grew some old types and some new ones — it took too much effort to slavishly follow the heritage-seed path.

Over the years the vegetable garden developed its own lore. Experience taught us that the best keeper potatoes are Bintjes, but the tastiest ones are Yukon Golds. While the old saying advises planting shallots and garlic at the winter solstice, those planted at the spring equinox will mature at more or less the same time. Nobody likes brussels sprouts, so it's best to grow them as an ornamental and give them to the chickens in the winter when they crave the greens. It is only a rumour that rhubarb is edible, but it is magnificent grown as an ornamental in the flower garden. There is always too much lettuce and cabbage. Organic broccoli heads often harbour a multitude of small worms that can be disconcerting to vegetarian and other squeamish guests. We can never grow and keep enough onions. Corn can be grown in unlimited amounts, because the chickens and the market lambs are willing to help eat it. Early Girl is a good tomato and ripens well on a windowsill. You will have many friends if you grow rows and rows of basil, and chickens are useful even when they're dead.

Winter

⟨+ +⟩

Keep the dry provender which you have laid up for winter and think
how long a winter it may be.   — Cato, 95-46 B.C.

THE WORST PART ABOUT WINTER, perhaps, is that you have to stay on
the farm. The days are short and the nights are long. It is as quiet as
a grave, and a farmer could be excused for wanting to take all his
livestock to the auction before abandoning the place for a warmer
clime.

Farmers who grow crops like wheat and get everything shipped
out by November are free to leave. As the joke goes: "Why is a
prairie farmer like a Boeing 747? Because they both whine all the
way to Hawaii." We could have set up our farm like that if we had
continued with Dave's rent-a-sheep operation and restricted ourselves to raising only meat chickens, but as soon as we decided to
have sustaining breeding flocks of sheep and laying hens we were
stuck. However, in return for our winter imprisonment, we got a
lot of pleasure from our animals during the other three and a half
seasons of the year. At least so far, it has been well worth the trade-
off, and besides, one has to have a time of the year for contempla-
tion and indoor tasks — there is certainly not much time for them
in the spring and the summer.

Our valley is usually quite mild in the winter, with no more than
an occasional snowfall and freeze-up, so the animals are able to
spend a lot of their time outside doing their thing, albeit on a more

limited basis than during the rest of the year. In much of the rest of North America, where winter arrives in November or December and sticks around without interruption until April, farming tasks are a routine that has been made much easier in recent years by machinery: electric heaters keep automatic waterers flowing; four-wheel-drive tractors with chains push snow out of the barnyard; the same tractor, fitted with a spike on its front-end loader, picks up a round hay bale weighing 100 kilograms or more and plunks it into a feeder, a far cry from the former task of hauling square bales through the snow to cattle and sheep. Many old barns were built against banks so that machinery had access to an upper floor that stored hay and grain, while the animals occupied a byre on a lower level and gravity did much of the work of moving feed around. Often the sun is bright, the air is clear and crisp, and the flies are dead. The farm chugs along steadily with few problems until the frost comes out of the ground in spring and turns the barnyard into a quagmire.

Quiet maintenance of the animals' health, and occasional maintenance of the property after winter storms, occupies the farmer throughout the winter. For small operators like us, whom freezing weather visits only sporadically, winter is considerably more work: the sheep have to be fed hay (about one kilogram a day each, in case you want to know) and, toward the end of the winter, when they're gaining weight just before lambing, grain; frozen buckets have to be emptied and filled and, when hoses freeze up, buckets have to be carried; and because the chickens spend a lot more time inside, sleeping through the 16-hour winter night, the coop has to be shovelled out every week.

As the light begins to fade at three or four in the afternoon, all the animals gather, just like feeding time at the zoo. The chickens, ducks, and geese wait around the doorway to the barn, where they know the grain is kept, and quack, honk, and croon; the sheep stand near the gate, where they can keep an eye on me, and baa and bawl.

Most of the barnyard decorum that stands them in good stead for the rest of the year vanishes when I begin to broadcast the grain—Arthur, the rooster, fends off any other species, including the geese that are three times his size, and hens squabble, but the ducks are smart enough to be led away into the former Fort Goose, where they are fed separately and then locked in. When I open their gate, the sheep charge in, scattering any chickens that have gotten in the way, but once at the grain feeders they settle down and even tolerate the occasional chicken that climbs in and pecks up bits of barley. In the winter, the shepherd can forego the rattling of the grain bucket when he needs his sheep and, instead, can use the age-old call, "Here, Sheep!" to bring them in. Throughout it all, there is more human-animal interaction, as it were: the animals recognize my value in the winter after having ignored me for most of the year. It is always nice to feel needed, even if it's just by sheep and poultry.

Of the livestock on our farm, only the chickens really feel the cold. They don't have any down, unlike the geese and ducks, and some days they get blown almost inside out. By minus 10 degrees they become quite disoriented, numbed and hunched; by minus 15, with additional windchill, even the geese and ducks spend all their time sitting quietly on their feet, keeping them warm. As long as the chickens can perch out of the wind, the only consequence of an extreme cold spell is the occasional grey spot of frostbite on their otherwise crimson combs. The sheep, with their long woolly coats, appear to enjoy the cold weather but get bored if they don't have grass to wander about on. At night they bury their heads in the fragrant hay and their contented munching is the only sound to be heard as the snow swirls about outside. As long as the winter temperature is steady, whatever it is, the animals cope, but if it swings wildly from above zero to far below, pneumonia can be a problem.

Winter also brings the predator population closer to the farm. Hunger makes them less cautious. On clear, cold, moonlit nights we are often awakened by the howling of a pack of coyotes in the woodlot a couple of hundred metres to the north. Eagles and hawks are much in evidence during the day, as is the heron that hunts along the edge of the pond. The barn owl, who lives in a nesting box high up at the back of the old hayloft, is out and flying at dusk; sometimes only its eerie screech reveals its presence, while other times we see its silhouette soaring across the starry sky. Gretchen the barn cat sleeps comfortably on the hay bales at a spot where she can survey a large part of the floor; her food comes to her on scurrying little feet, looking for warmth and spilled grain away from the snow and the wet fields.

Every chicken farmer agrees that the worst predators are mink: long, narrow killing machines like furred snakes. They are renowned for killing in a frenzy of blood-lust, and if they get into an enclosed coop they might make a pile of 60 or more dead chickens. "These are mine," their behaviour says, "and I'll do something with them later." Although there are few wild mink in our valley, there are quite a number of mink ranches — fur may go in and out of fashion, but mink always appears to be a fairly profitable cash crop. One autumn a group of animal-rights activists released several thousand mink from a ranch a few kilometres from us. Even though most were recaptured or died in the unfamiliar surroundings of Mother Nature, everyone raising free-range chickens went instantly on high alert. Ironically, because of the mink "liberation," the only chickens in the valley that were safe were the ones kept indoors in captivity.

For a couple of weeks I kept the chickens locked in their run, a fenced area of about 10 by five metres; at night they were able to go in through a low door to the coop and its perches and emerge again in the morning to pace restlessly back and forth along the fence and wonder, as chickens are wont to do, why they couldn't be outside. Eventually both they and I tired of the situation; I figured any mink would likely strike at night, and I made sure all the chickens were in with the door into the run latched at dusk. The weeks passed without incident.

One cold winter morning, as part of the day's routine, I went down to the run to let the chickens out and discovered three hens in a most curious position, their heads together in what appeared to be a small hole in the fence. Their dead bodies were entirely unmarked, with not even a dishevelled feather, but their necks had been cleaned of feathers and their heads were partly eaten. Three of them! I phoned Jan. "Mink," was all he said. I thought if I patched the hole and systematically hardened the target, as the security people say, I could force the mink to move on.

Two nights later it struck again — this time two birds were stuck headfirst into another tiny hole, one whose size I had misjudged, through which the mink evidently had tried to pull them. They had the same ghastly disfigurement of the head and neck. It was tempting to salvage their bodies for the stockpot, but I didn't know how long they had been dead, so they were regretfully consigned whole to the garden. That night I closed the inner door — the one that connected the coop with the fenced run. Surely *this* will move it along, I hoped.

A couple of days passed. It was about 10 o'clock in the morning when I happened to look out of the house down across the barnyard toward the coop and saw the hens all gathered around Arthur in a tight little knot, like they do when there's a hawk in the sky. But there wasn't a hawk to be seen. I opened the door to listen. From the coop came the sound of a chicken clucking loudly. I put on my boots and ran down.

When I opened the door into the coop, the first thing I saw was the hen that had been making all the noise; absolutely terrified, her eyes glazed with fear and open wide, she stood frozen on the perch. On the floor underneath the nesting boxes was another chicken, on its side and twitching. I peered into the gloom. The mink, sleek and dark brown, was biting at the chicken's neck and lapping at the blood that welled up from it.

Stepping quickly inside, I grabbed the live chicken by the feet. It shrieked, poor thing, a terrible sound I had never heard a chicken make before. I retreated, closing the door behind me, and took my panicked catch back to the rest of the chickens, dropped her beside them on the ground, and ran back to the barn to get my pellet gun. By the time I returned the mink had escaped. So much for nocturnal attacks. I took the dead chicken and, thinking that at least *she* was not going to be wasted, cut her head off and began to clean her for soup stock. Inside her was a perfectly formed egg, ready to be laid: she was obviously pock-pock-pocking her way into her favourite nesting box when the mink grabbed her.

The severed head was saved for the trap that I immediately went to the co-op to buy: a live trap called a HAVAHART, the idea being that the trapped animal can be humanely released elsewhere. The mink obligingly walked into it that same afternoon, whereupon I, being in a take-no-prisoners mood, shot it. Thrifty as always, which I attribute to my Scottish mother, I skinned it and, using a recipe for tanning solution from one of Christine's Australian countrywomen's cookbooks, treated the pelt. After it cured, I presented it to Christine, probably the only mink she'll ever get. Alive it had been a beautiful, evil little creature, about half a metre long and thin like a tube. Some months later a visitor to the house identified it as a wild mink, not one of the survivors from the nearby "liberation."

Most predator attacks are not so stressful. One Christmas morning Chuck called, wished us best of the season, and told us that he could see a coyote at the top of our pasture with something in its mouth. "Through the binoculars, it looks like one of those black-and-white stripey chickens — that's the kind you've got, isn't it?" I wished him and Angela a merry Christmas and went back to presents and eggnog. Peace on earth and goodwill to all predators. An hour later we walked up to the top of the field and found only a pile of black-and-white feathers and a few scraps of beak and feet

on the wet grass. The coyote had come for its Christmas dinner
and left by burrowing under the fence at a soft spot. I got a wheelbarrow full of rocks and plugged the hole.

The Return of Spring

⟵ ⁺ ⟶

Without forage no cattle; without cattle no manure; without manure
no crops.   — old Flemish proverb

IN THE CITY, and in much of modern animal husbandry, one season moves seamlessly into the next, illuminated by electric light and
enclosed by walls. "Everything comes and goes / marked by lovers
and styles of clothes," wrote Joni Mitchell. By contrast, traditional
agriculture, for all its hard work and meagre rewards, connects the
human animal with the so-called lesser ones that are still plugged
into the rhythms of the planet. On the farm, even the simplest tasks
gain greater meaning because they are part of the cosmic cycle. On
second thought, I think that's just a rationalization. I'll try restating
it: old-fashioned farms have their own rhythm, which is sometimes
meaningful and other times is a straitjacket. "Do you live on a hobby
farm?" well-meaning people have asked. "No, it's a forced-labour
camp," I'm provoked to reply.

The change of the seasons is never more evident than when the
earth begins to shift from the tranquillity of winter. With the onset
of spring the pace quickens. The chickens return to full egg production and, as they contemplate motherhood, become ever more
devious at hiding their eggs. The ducks swim about in arabesques
before stopping face to face; they bob their heads in courtship,
before the drake jumps on top of the hen, forcing her underwater
for what seems like an eternity. The geese become remarkably docile

and dreamily arrange heaps of straw into nests with their beaks. The sheep stand in the sun with their noses lifted in the air toward the scent of spring. The frogs emerge from their hibernation in the mud and begin to croak. Songbirds nest, and raucous Canada geese pass through on their way north.

At the barn, when we get a mild spell in February, we corral the sheep and spend half a day picking the straw and hay from their fleeces. Then Geoff the shearer comes by, bringing with him his son-in-law Pat who is learning the shearing trade and has a strong young back. The sheep, released of six or seven kilograms of wool, spend the next day inside — shivering a little and nuzzling down in the extra straw that has been provided — but quickly grow a nubbly coat and bound around like lambs, sometimes hopping on all fours, other times kicking up their heels. I set up the lambing "jugs" within the wider pen at least a month before the first lambs are due, because the ewes, as their lambs begin to grow inside them and they begin to "bag out," are already choosing the places where they will lamb — when their water breaks, they will push aside any hindrance that is between them and their spot. They spend a lot of time chewing their cuds; each wad of cud comes up from the rumen — you can see it, a lump travelling up the neck to the mouth — and is chewed about 60 times, plus or minus five or so, before being swallowed again and replaced by another bit. Old sheep in familiar surroundings are very thoughtful and systematic.

FOR OUR LITTLE PLACE, we arrived at a balance of about 20 ewes and a ram — they have enough room to move around and grass to eat, the old box stalls on the ground floor of the barn are big enough to hold 120 bales of hay, and the work of foot trimming, worming, vaccinating, and dagging (cleaning up their bum wool) is only aging me at a pace I can live with. We have enough fleeces for the customers and vice versa — the best of the wool is bought by hand-spinners and weavers, while the balance becomes a tiny part of the wool shipment from the sheep in our valley to a mill in Alberta — usually two semi-trailer loads of baled, compacted wool to be turned into socks and blankets and felts.

Conversation among shepherds often dwells on rams, as everyone needs to introduce a new purebred bloodline from time to time or wants to crossbreed, usually to produce more prolific and faster-growing meat sheep. Although incest is okay for a generation or two, and can reinforce the characteristics you want in your flock, eventually you need a new ram (just like you need a new rooster) to keep your flock from becoming like the Irish potato crop of the 1840s. In our case, Eric's first boy was with Gladys, who had a great fleece, and he was one of triplets, which is an inheritable trait like good fleece; Jan thought he was a handsome little guy, so we kept him and named him Eddie, after the bridegroom at the wedding that took place on the evening he was born. Eddie and Eric spent a couple of years together, separated from the ewes except for the month of breeding when we divided the ewes up between them. The two rams got along quite well, with only the occasional pushing and shoving and butting to confirm Eric's role as the dominant male. Most days, Eddie in effect said, "Hey, Dad, let's go eat a little grass!" and so together they spent much quality time. Eventually, though, old Eric lost his dominant role to his son and then developed hoof problems and a bit of arthritis, so he had to be shipped for shepherd's sausage, as the expression puts it. As for Eddie, he grew into a fine ram and has fathered many lambs, some with his mother and sisters and daughters, but will soon need a new place of employment. Maybe we'll be able to do a trade.

But it isn't always that simple: the real concern with bringing in new animals is the invisible stuff — the diseases and genetic abnormalities and combinations — they might bring with them. Some are quite minor and get "turned up" by the breeding combination like a playing card cut from a deck; one such is entropion, a curiously

126

rolled eyelid with the eyelash chafing the lamb's eyeball and eventually blinding it. It is relatively easily fixed by sewing the eyelid to the
cheek for a couple of days until it grows naturally, but pushing a
needle and thread through a lamb's eyelid can be a bit disconcerting. Such a lamb, needless to say, is marked for culling.

Getting new animals is rather like buying a used car and wondering what repairs you might be up for. When you buy an animal from
an acquaintance or a friend, you can be pretty sure you know the history of your new purchase and whether the farm has anything circu-
lating — like foot rot or mastitis or lymphadenitis — that you might
bring home. By comparison, buying animals at the country auction
is a little like shopping at the used-car lot, with the fast-talking auctioneer in his western shirt and bolo tie behaving just a little like the
commission salesman with the friendly smile, warm handshake, and
plaid suit.

You know you've adjusted from city life to farm life when you
can go to the auction without either getting depressed or wanting to
save all the animals for sale there. The auction is *reality*, in contrast
to the easygoing routine on a farm like ours where most of the animals go about their business for years. The animal auction in our
nearby town takes place every Saturday morning and is the big one
for the whole valley; on a side road next to a farm-equipment
dealer, the auction buildings include a number of fenced pens and
loading docks, and an open area where cages of poultry and bunnies
are set out for viewing, all under a broad roof. A great variety of the
farm population, *agricola vulgaris*, attends: rough-looking men in
overalls and gum boots buy pigs and cattle (and lambs when available) to fatten for the market; teenagers from the 4-H Clubs look
for animals to buy, or sell the ones that were their project during the
previous year, and divide their time between watching the old farmers and teasing and flirting with each other; men and women in
clean clothes and city shoes check through the poultry cages for a
peacock to replace the one they just lost to a coyote; hard-eyed Asian

men in ball caps and checked shirts note the tag numbers on the cages of ducks.

Anyone who wants to bid on one of the lots, which might be a cage of sweaty Cornish Giant chickens or an enormous pig, registers at the office, gets a paddle with a bidding number, and proceeds to the auction hall itself, an amphitheatre of tiers of benches ascending steeply, like the cheap seats in an old-fashioned theatre, to the ceiling. At the front, beside a small display area, the auctioneer and recorder sit. Perhaps a hundred people, mostly men segregated into their respective ethnic groups, pack the room and strain their ears to follow the characteristic machine-gun patter of the auctioneer. As each lot is announced (if it is a portable set of critters), one of the farm-wise boys or girls who work the viewing area outside carries in the cage and holds it up, sometimes pulling out a rooster or a rabbit and holding it high for everyone to see. The bidding goes back and forth in a blur; some players are obviously professionals, perhaps buying game birds for restaurants or, like Dave Thompson (of the rent-a-sheep operation), putting together flocks of animals for grazing contracts. Outside in the parking lot, other farmers sell eggs and vegetables from the backs of their pickups; an old Italian guy, in defiance of marketing boards and health regulations, sells his homemade cheese; sometimes flat decks loaded with hay are parked along the edge of the lot, offering instant free delivery to anyone who will take the load. Everyone walks around carrying steaming coffee in a Styrofoam cup.

The proverbial bottom line of farming is to produce the maximum weight of crop off the available acreage. When it comes right down to it, everything else, including the pleasure nearly every farmer takes from his land and his animals, is a frill. Although lambs are unbelievably cute when they're little, after about four months they become teenagers and, like their human counterparts, are rarely lovable or tolerable. The boys are especially pesky and divide their time between head-butting among themselves and mounting any of their contemporaries (whether male or female), riding around on each other's backs and playing at being grown up. To grow them out properly to market size they need to be sheared and then fed on the best grass or grain, and as they push and shove and sort out their order of dominance the shepherd begins to consider the best way of turning them into cash.

For us, taking lambs to the auction was one way; another was calling Dave during periods of high lamb prices when it was profitable for him to buy feeder lambs. A third way was through a neighbour, Terry, from the next street to the south, who raised a few sheep himself on a couple of shady acres and who often jogged down our road pushing a stroller containing his daughter. He worked for the telephone company and, among his friends and numerous colleagues, always had more lamb customers than he could supply. So he would come by, in his big pickup truck with the fibreglass box on the back, pay cash for any lambs I had, and then take them away. It was easy, especially for me. The lambs had had a happy, if brief, life; here for a good time if not a long time, as the song put it.

However, after a year or two I had my own customers and had to start taking lambs to the abattoir. It seemed like a grim thing to do: you ship them empty, meaning you cut off the food supply 12 hours or so before, and only give them a handful of hay at dawn so they'll get on the truck happy. The abattoir accepted lambs and goats only one day of the week, between five and eight in the morning, and I steeled myself for that day and didn't sleep well the night before. But, as had been the case with the beheading of Yum Yum the chicken, the lambs seemed less bothered by the procedure than I was. Poor little trusting bastards, I thought.

Loaded into the pickup, they were calm and not at all stressed as I drove through the countryside toward Pine Ridge Processors, a family-run operation that had been in business for a couple of generations. In the early morning light the grey building looked especially purposeful, with only a few lights showing from what was evidently the human entrance. Signs shouted directions to the unloading area: BACK IN ONLY, said one; ABSOLUTELY NO UNLOADING WITHOUT PERMISSION, said another. In the gloom of the loading dock, a young guy with long hair, smoking a cigarette and wearing a bloodstained apron, directed me in; he glanced into the back of the pickup, probably to make sure everyone was healthy and alive, then told me to wait a minute. Moving a gate aside, he returned to the holding pen at the dock and walked smoothly among the goats and sheep that had already been delivered, tagging the ears of the ones that were unidentified and writing numbers on a form that he handed back to the couple of farmers who were waiting and had already unloaded their trucks. Throughout it all he was quiet and businesslike, speaking to animal and human alike in a low voice. I had envisaged shouting men, bright lights, pens of animals lathered with sweaty fear, and lowing cattle with wild eyes, but it was not like that. The goats and sheep looked back at me rather blankly — puzzled maybe, but hardly panicked. My lambs came down out of the truck to join the throng, and the young man scribbled a number on the pad of forms, tore the top one off, and handed it to me. The only definable sound in the background was an occasional loud click, probably from the killing gun, probably the sort of captive-piston arrangement that is quick and economical and ...whatever. I didn't want to know, and I went quickly into the office with my form and gave directions to the attendant to have the carcasses shipped to a butcher close to home. It's tough to feel like a hobby farmer if you're taking lambs to the slaughter.

JOHN HEYWOOD'S EPIGRAM — "When the sunne shineth, make hay" — is true, metaphorically, for this sort of farming life. You have to have the freedom to do the farming work when it needs to be done, rather than when you can find the time to do it, and the patience and flexibility to do other things when the weather is awful or when nobody needs any attention. Every day is a little bit different from the previous one, but generally you only need to find a few minutes here and there for the different groups of animals, the fences, the fields, and the garden. In this scale of farming, there is usually enough time to sit back and smell the roses and, indeed, to earn some of the city money that everyone needs nowadays. After all, you don't have to watch the animals eat. But there is always the temptation to try something new — hmm, everything's working smoothly now, so maybe we should get some new animals. Where could we put a pig? How about llamas? Maybe a couple of dozen bronze turkeys?

In the final analysis, for us moving to the farm was the right decision for the time, because we can no longer imagine living anywhere else. This sort of thing is presumed to be a retirement project — an alternative to the golf course or Winnebago — and perhaps is just that for those people with enough money to get the heavy work done by others, or to buy a place that's all set up. Maybe when we're older we'll feel differently, and we'll sell to someone young who can enjoy the fruits of *our* folly, as Cato put it. But we're glad we didn't wait. After all, retirement is too important to leave for old age.

Bibliography

⟨+ +⟩

The following books were used as references or were quoted from in the text.

Bonham-Carter, Victor. *The English Village.* Harmondsworth, Eng.: Penguin Books, 1952.

Carpenter, Frank George. *How the World Is Fed: Readers on Commerce and Industry.* New York: American Book Company, 1907.

Clark, Geo H., and M. Oscar Malte. *Fodder and Pasture Plants.* Ottawa: Dominion of Canada, Department of Agriculture, 1913.

Hertzberg, Ruth, Beatrice Vaughan, and Janet Greene. *Putting Food By.* Brattleboro, VT: Stephen Greene Press, 1973.

Howard, Sir Albert. *An Agricultural Testament.* New York: Oxford University Press, 1943.

Hughes, James Laughlin, and Ellsworth D. Foster, eds. *The Dominion Educator.* Toronto: P. D. Palmer, 1923. *An encyclopedia for Canadian high school students.*

Mercia, Leonard S. *Raising Poultry the Modern Way.* Pownal, VT: Garden Way Publishing, 1975.

Rennie, William, Sr. *Rennie's Agriculture in Canada: Modern Principles of Agriculture Applicable to Canadian Farming to Yield Greater Profit.* Toronto: William Rennie Company, 1916.

Smith, Page, and Charles Daniel. *The Chicken Book.* Boston: Little, Brown, 1975. *This book is a classic: a course on the chicken, taught at Cowell College, University of California, Santa Cruz, in the middle of chicken country in the spring of 1972. It put together a scientist-biologist with a humanist-historian around a topic — the chicken — and investigated it as a subject of folklore, history, science, anthropology, agriculture, and cuisine. They found that during their academic excursion they were following, "quite unwittingly, in the footsteps of the great Italian Renaissance natural historian Ulisse Aldrovandi, who, like us, insisted on perceiving the chicken as part of a much larger 'order of things.'"*

Starr, Kevin. *Endangered Dreams: The Great Depression in California.* New York: Oxford University Press, 1996.

Trager, James. *The Food Chronology.* New York: Henry Holt, 1995. *The history of the world told through food and drink.*

Warren, G. F. *Farm Management.* New York: Macmillan, 1913. *Part of the Rural Text Book Series.*

Waters, Henry Jackson. *The New Agriculture.* Boston: Ginn and Company, 1924. *A textbook for high school students.*

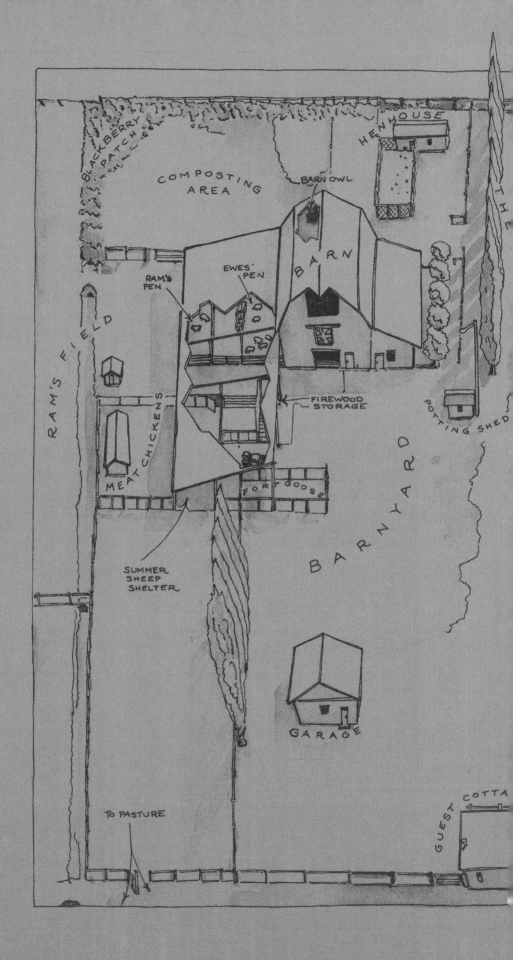